D0220424

NRAEF ManageFirst
Managerial Accounting
Competency Guide

National Restaurant Association
EDUCATIONAL FOUNDATION
175 West Jackson Boulevard, Suite 1500
Chicago, IL 60604-2814
www.nraef.org
©2006 The National Restaurant Association Educational Foundation

Pearson
Prentice
Hall

Upper Saddle River, New Jersey 07458

National Restaurant Association
EDUCATIONAL FOUNDATION

Disclaimer

Table of Contents

A Message from the National Restaurant Association Educational Foundation

The National Restaurant Association Educational Foundation (NRAEF) is a not-for-profit organization dedicated to fulfilling the educational mission of the National Restaurant Association. We focus on helping the restaurant and foodservice industry address its risk management, recruitment, and retention challenges.

As the nation's largest private-sector employer, the restaurant, hospitality, and foodservice industry is the cornerstone of the American economy, of career-and-employment opportunities, and of local communities. The total economic impact of the restaurant industry is astounding—representing approximately 10 percent of the U.S. gross domestic product. At the NRAEF, we are focused on enhancing this position by providing the valuable tools and resources needed to educate our current and future professionals.

For more information on the NRAEF, please visit our Web site at *www.nraef.org.*

What is the NRAEF ManageFirst Program?

The NRAEF ManageFirst Program is a management-training certificate program that exemplifies our commitment to developing materials by the industry, for the industry. The program's most powerful strength is that it is based on a set of competencies defined by the restaurant, foodservice, and hospitality industry as critical for success.

NRAEF ManageFirst Program Components

The NRAEF ManageFirst Program includes a set of competency guides, exams, instructor resources, certificates, a new credential, and support activities and services. By participating in the program, you are demonstrating your commitment to becoming a highly qualified professional either preparing to begin or to advance your career in the restaurant, hospitality, and foodservice industry.

The competency guides cover the range of topics listed in the chart at right.

Competency Guide/Exam Topics

NRAEF ManageFirst Core Credential Topics

Hospitality and Restaurant Management

Controlling Foodservice Costs

Human Resources Management and Supervision

ServSafe Food Safety

NRAEF ManageFirst Foundation Topics

Managerial Accounting

Inventory and Purchasing

Customer Service

Food Production

Menu Marketing and Management

Restaurant Marketing

Nutrition

ServSafe Alcohol Responsible Alcohol Service

Within the guides, you will find the essential content for the topic as defined by industry, as well as learning activities, assessments, case studies, suggested field projects, professional profiles, and testimonials. You will also find an answer sheet for an NRAEF exam written specifically for each topic. The exam can be administered either online or in a paper and pencil format, and it will be proctored. Upon successfully passing the exam, you will be furnished by the NRAEF with a customized certificate. The certificate is a lasting recognition of your accomplishment and a signal to the industry that you have mastered the competency covered within the particular topic.

To earn the NRAEF's new credential, you will be required to pass four core exams and one foundation exam (to be chosen from the remaining program topics) and to document your work experience in the restaurant and foodservice industry. Earning the NRAEF credential is a significant accomplishment.

We applaud you as you begin or advance your career in the restaurant, hospitality, and foodservice industry. Visit *www.nraef.org* to learn about additional career-building resources offered by the NRAEF, including scholarships for college students enrolled in relevant industry programs.

NRAEF ManageFirst Program Ordering Information

Review copies or support materials:
FACULTY FIELD SERVICES
800.526.0485

Domestic orders and inquiries:
PEARSON CUSTOMER SERVICE
Tel: 800.922.0579
www.prenhall.com

International orders and inquiries:
U.S. EXPORT SALES OFFICE
Pearson Education International Customer Service Group
200 Old Tappan Road
Old Tappan, NJ 07675 USA
Tel: 201.767.5021
Fax: 201.767.5625

For corporate, government and special sales (consultants, corporations, training centers, VARs, and corporate resellers) orders and inquiries:
PEARSON CORPORATE SALES
Phone: 317.428.3411
Fax: 317.428.3343
Email: managefirst@prenhall.com

For additional information regarding other Prentice Hall publications, instructor and student support materials, locating your sales representative and much more, please visit *www.prenhall.com/managefirst.*

Acknowledgements

The National Restaurant Association Educational Foundation is grateful for the expertise and guidance of our many advisors, subject matter experts, reviewers, and other contributors.

We are pleased to thank the following people for their time, effort, and dedication to this program.

Ernest Boger	Thomas Kaltenecker	James Perry
Robert Bosselman	Ray Kavanaugh	William N. Reynolds
Jerald Chesser	John Kidwell	Rosenthal Group
Cynthia Deale	Carol Kizer	Mokie Steiskal
Fred DeMicco	Fred Mayo	Karl Titz
John Drysdale	Cynthia Mayo	Terry Umbreit
Gene Fritz	Patrick Moreo	Deanne Williams
John Gescheidle	Robert O'Halloran	Mike Zema
Thomas Hamilton	Brian O'Malley	
John Hart	Terrence Pappas	

Features of the NRAEF ManageFirst Competency Guides

We have designed the NRAEF ManageFirst Competency Guides to enhance your ability to learn and retain important information that is critical to this restaurant and foodservice industry function. Here are the key features you will find within this guide.

Beginning Each Guide

Tuning In to You

When you open an NRAEF ManageFirst Competency Guide for the first time, you might ask yourself: Why do I need to know about this topic? Every topic of these guides involves key information you will be need as you manage a restaurant or foodservice operation. Located in the front of each review guide, "Tuning In to You" is a brief synopsis that illustrates some of the reasons the information contained throughout that particular guide is important to you. It exemplifies real-life scenarios that you will face as a manager and how the concepts in the book will help you in your career.

Professional Profile

This is your opportunity to meet a professional who is currently working in the field associated with a competency guide's topic. This person's story will help you gain insight into the responsibilities related to his or her position, as well as the training and educational history linked to it. You will also see the daily and cumulative impact this position has on an operation, and receive advice from a person who has successfully met the challenges of being a manager.

Beginning Each Chapter

Inside This Chapter

Chapter content is organized under these major headings.

Learning Objectives

Learning objectives identify what you should be able to do after completing each chapter. These objectives are linked to the required tasks a manager must be able to perform in relation to the function discussed in the competency guide.

Test Your Knowledge

Each chapter begins with some True or False questions designed to test your prior knowledge of some of the concepts presented in the chapter. The answers to these questions, as well as the concepts behind them, can be found within the chapter—see the page reference after each question.

Key Terms

These terms are important for thorough understanding of the chapter's content. They are highlighted throughout the chapter, where they are explicitly defined or their meaning is made clear within the paragraphs in which they appear.

Throughout Each Chapter

Exhibits

Exhibits are placed throughout each chapter to visually reinforce the key concepts presented in the text. Types of exhibits include charts, tables, photographs, and illustrations.

Think About It. . .

These thought-provoking sidebars reveal supportive information about the section they appear beside.

Activities

Apply what you have learned throughout the chapter by completing the various activities in the text. The activities have been designed to give you additional practice and better understanding of the concepts addressed in the learning objectives. Types of activities include case studies, role-plays, and problem solving, among others.

Exhibit

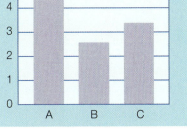

Exhibits are visuals that will help you learn about key concepts.

Think About It...

Consider these supplemental insights as you read through a chapter.

Activity

Activity

Types of activities you will complete include case studies, role-plays, and problem solving, among others.

At the End of Each Chapter

Review Your Learning

These multiple-choice or open- or close-ended questions or problems are designed to test your knowledge of the concepts presented in the chapter. These questions have been aligned with the objectives and should provide you with an opportunity to practice or apply the content that supports these objectives. If you have difficulty answering them, you should review the content further.

At the End of the Guide

Field Project

This real-world project gives you the valuable opportunity to apply many of the concepts you will learn in a competency guide. You will interact with industry practitioners, enhance your knowledge, and research, apply, analyze, evaluate, and report on your findings. It will provide you with an in-depth "reality check" of the policies and practices of this management function.

Tuning In to You

Crrraaaaanggg!!!!

At a café, the dishwasher loses a teaspoon down the drain of a sink and accidentally turns on the garbage disposal. The spoon is recovered, but it is a mangled mess of metal. It is unusable. Well, the spoon only costs $5.00 to replace, but to generate enough profit to buy the replacement spoon, the business will have to sell $80.65 in additional sales. Think that number is too large? It's not.

Because of the expenses involved in running a foodservice operation, most restaurants have profit margins that are very small. What does this mean? This means that only a small percentage of each dollar of sales is actually profit. The rest goes to pay for food, supplies, labor, utilities, insurance, and other costs of running the business. In the competitive business of running a restaurant or foodservice operation, you can see why following well-established accounting routines is critical to keeping the business afloat.

Restaurant and foodservice managers make important decisions every day based on financial information. As a manager, you too will be responsible for the profitability and financial health of an operation. Losing a few dollars from the drawer or forgetting to pay a bill on time may seem like an inevitable aspect of running a business. You might be thinking that, realistically, there will be times when change is not handled properly or a bill is lost in the shuffle. And you aren't wrong. But well-organized cash handling and accounting procedures reduce the likelihood of these mishaps.

Although managing an operation's finances might be intimidating at first, you will learn the basics to get started on the right foot. Most important is to not underestimate the amount of care that must go into managing day-to-day accounting practices. Ensuring sound financial business practices throughout the operation results in protected revenue and increased profit for the organization.

Professional Profile
Your opportunity to meet someone working in the field

Maria Simmons, RD, LDN

Patient Foodservice Manager
Swedish Covenant Hospital
Chicago, IL

I always thought I would become a doctor. I began my college studies as a premedicine major at Illinois Wesleyan University in Bloomington, Illinois. My mother was seriously ill and passed away, and I returned to Chicago, my hometown, to help care for my younger brother and sister. I came to realize that I no longer wanted to be a medical doctor.

I was still very interested in the sciences, however, and wanted to continue my education closer to home. So I transferred to the University of Illinois at Chicago (UIC) and applied to its nutrition program. This program is extremely competitive and admits only eighteen new students every year. I had to go through a process of interviews and essay writing in order to be accepted—and I made it in! At UIC, I earned a Bachelor of Science degree in Medical Dietetics and Nutrition.

Throughout the course of my studies, the kitchen management and food production courses always interested me the most. I started my professional career in 1987 as a supervisor for Northwestern Memorial Hospital in Chicago. One year later, I was promoted to coordinator over all the supervisors at the hospital, and I held that position for seven more years.

Although I enjoyed the hospital's environment, I was given the opportunity to explore a position with more impact on the community. Through the Chicago Urban League, I became a community dietician at a Head Start clinic. There I was involved on a daily basis with young mothers and their babies, reinforcing the important lessons of nutrition, health, and cleanliness. This was such a rewarding position! Every day I saw the impact of my work on these young lives. Unfortunately, funding for several positions was discontinued, and I had to move on.

In 1998, I started working at Swedish Covenant Hospital. I walked into a community hospital foodservice kitchen where time had stood still. The kitchen's meal tray system had been developed in 1976 and was outdated and costly to use. There was a lot of work to be done.

So how do I use managerial accounting in my job?

As the department manager, I supervise an annual budget of more than two million dollars. A third of that amount is food cost. Our food budget has increased by about 10 percent in the past year. Most of this increase is due to new programs featuring specialized food, nutritional supplements, and organic food. My team and I want to be on the cutting edge when it comes to offering our patients the highest quality, healthiest food available at a time when they need it the most. We have implemented several different menu options that appeal to our patients' diverse dietary needs and cultural preferences, including Korean, Indian-Halal, and Hispanic meals.

I also oversee the staffing budget for patient foodservices. Every year I calculate projections based on a fiscal year that begins on October 1. I base this budget on the number of work hours anticipated, the number of hours that are productive, and the number of positions to staff each day—all of which is based on a master schedule. Over the past seven years, my staff has increased from forty-two to forty-six full-time equivalents. Our service standard is currently three meal trays per minute, so that is the labor productivity target we shoot for every day. I also budget for on-call staff and agency staff to handle temporary staffing needs.

In addition, I have to plan for capital spending for the department. Reworking the tray system, for example, involves purchasing all new components—trays, plates, underliners, lids, and equipment for warming, holding, and transporting meals. In addition, we have upgraded large production equipment such as steamers, kettles, and stoves. Over the past seven years, the department has spent between $30,000 and $50,000 annually on capital improvements.

My staff members review and approve all the invoices that come through the patient foodservices department. Every month, the hospital finance department provides a report of how much my department has spent. I review these reports and compare them to my budget. Whenever the numbers appear out of line, I look into what might be causing this, and what I can do to bring those costs back in line.

As you can see, managing finances takes a lot of my time, but it is very important to all the aspects of this department. It is especially important to ensuring that the patients—our customers—receive the best service and food during their stay in our hospital.

Managing Cash at the Operation

After completing this chapter, you should be able to:

- Describe best practices for monitoring cash handling at the operation.
- Calculate guest checks, including tax and tip amounts.
- Process cash and noncash payments received from guests.
- Store cash and noncash receipts securely.
- Perform cash register reconciliation.
- Prepare a bank deposit.

Test Your Knowledge

■ **True or False:** There are no reliable ways to monitor cash handling at most foodservice operations. *(See pp. 2–3.)*

■ **True or False:** The amount left as a tip is usually determined by the customer. *(See p. 4.)*

■ **True or False:** Several U.S. currency denominations include security features that help cashiers determine the bills' authenticity. *(See p. 5.)*

■ **True or False:** Change should be given in the smallest denominations available. *(See p. 8.)*

■ **True or False:** Credit cards should never be accepted without first requesting an additional form of identification. *(See p. 10.)*

Key Terms

Bleed

Gratuity

Reconciliation

Security feature

Subtotal

Variance

Introduction

To properly manage a restaurant, there must be guidelines in place to ensure responsible handling of cash and other payments. Basic math skills and attention to detail are important in calculating guest checks, receiving payments from guests, and making change. The guidelines for managing cash listed in this chapter are a good starting point for any operation. Many operations already have their own procedures in place as well.

The Importance of Monitoring

It is a manager's job to ensure that any procedures related to handling cash are properly trained and enforced. There are three common ways to monitor how employees handle cash:

■ **Manage by walking around.** Let your employees see you and know that you are around, both to help them and to coach them. If you see an employee not following procedure, point it out to him or her and explain how to correct the problem.

2 **Monitor with a surveillance system.** Closed-circuit cameras are a great way to detect improper cash handling, including theft. If there is a dispute about what size bill the customer gave the employee, you can quickly play back the surveillance tape and correct the situation with visual proof. Just having cameras around can also be a deterrent for employees to be careless or to consider stealing.

3 **Hire secret shoppers.** There are services available that send hired "customers" into the restaurant to check the service level of your employees. These "customers" then give a thorough report about every interaction that occurred during their visit. This is a great way to monitor your employees without them changing their behavior, as they might when a manager is present.

Calculating Guest Checks

In today's high-tech foodservice industry, most guest check calculations are automated and computerized. It is rare to see an old cash register in a modern restaurant. Foodservice managers will seldom need to calculate guest checks by hand unless there is a POS equipment malfunction or they happen to be working in a remote or lower-tech location. When faced with such realities, it is critical to understand what goes into the accurate calculation of guest checks.

Calculating Subtotal

When calculating a guest check, all of the listed items are added together, resulting in a subtotal. It is sometimes necessary to first separate the items into different categories, such as by food or beverage. This might be done for record-keeping or tax calculation purposes. For example, beverages with alcohol might be taxed at a higher percentage than those without alcohol.

Calculating Sales Tax

Sales tax, if applicable, is then added to the subtotal. To calculate the sales tax, multiply the subtotal by the percentage of sales tax required by state and local law. Make sure you are aware of any applicable laws when calculating sales tax to ensure correct values. In the sample guest check on p. 4, the sales tax is 6 percent. This means that the subtotal of $17.50 is multiplied by 0.06 to calculate the sales tax. Then the sales tax of $1.05 is added to the subtotal to create the total the customer must pay.

Exhibit 1a

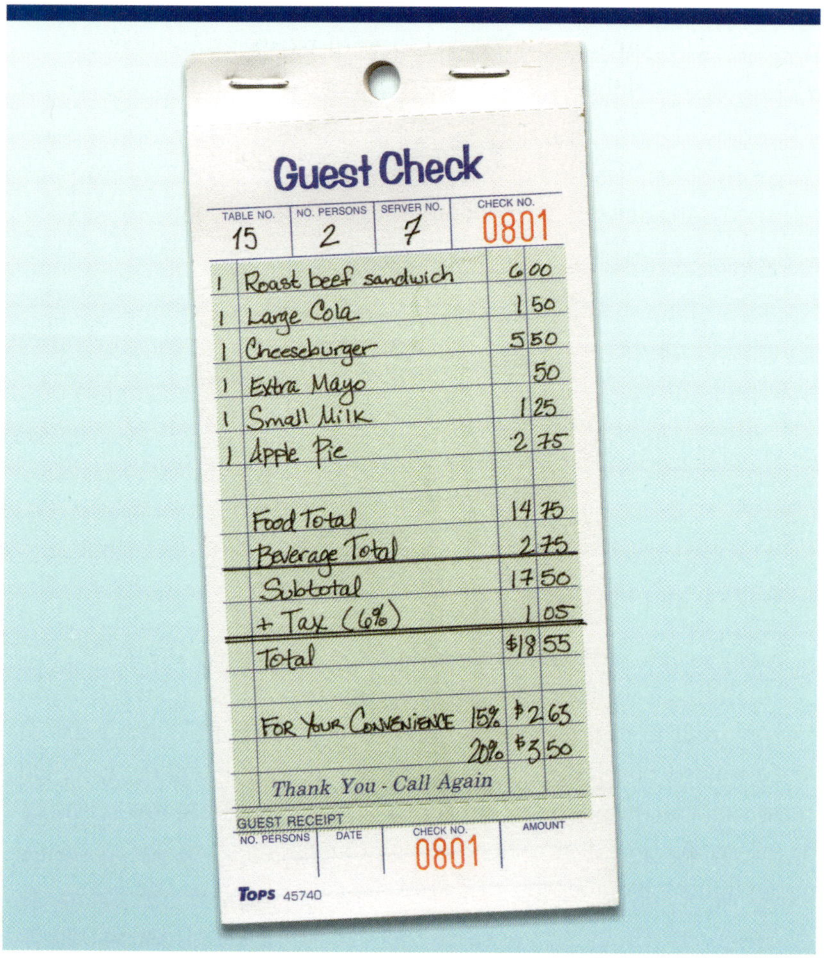

Sample guest check

Calculating Gratuity

Most of the time, the amount of gratuity—or tip—is left to the customer's discretion. In the United States, it is customary to tip a server an amount equal to 15 to 20 percent of the check subtotal. There are circumstances, however, where the tip is included in the check total. Some restaurants automatically add a gratuity to larger parties (usually six or more people). Operations that have a high amount of international tourists will automatically include a gratuity on checks to avoid customers not tipping because of customary differences.

In the sample guest check in *Exhibit 1a*, tip calculations for both 15 percent and 20 percent are provided at the bottom of the check to give the customer a recommended tip range.

Many people also carry wallet-sized charts, or tip tables, to help them quickly determine an appropriate tip. An example of a tip table is shown in *Exhibit 1b*.

Processing Payment from Guests

Satisfied guests pay for their dining experiences through a variety of types of transactions—including both cash and noncash payment options. Depending on the operation, guests might pay their checks through interaction with different employees—from servers, to cashiers, to bartenders. These transactions usually take place without incident. At the same time, it is important for all employees to understand the best practices for processing payments from guests.

Processing Cash Payments

Cash is the most widely accepted form of payment. However, handling actual currency comes with its own set of concerns. Being familiar with the different bills and coins that make up U.S. currency will go a long way toward processing cash payments accurately.

Exhibit 1b

Tip Table

Check Subtotal	15%	18%	20%
$ 5.00	0.75	0.90	1.00
$ 10.00	1.50	1.80	2.00
$ 15.00	2.25	2.70	3.00
$ 20.00	3.00	3.60	4.00
$ 25.00	3.75	4.50	5.00
$ 30.00	4.50	5.40	6.00
$ 35.00	5.25	6.30	7.00
$ 40.00	6.00	7.20	8.00
$ 45.00	6.75	8.10	9.00
$ 50.00	7.50	9.00	10.00
$ 60.00	9.00	10.80	12.00
$ 70.00	10.50	12.60	14.00
$ 80.00	12.00	14.40	16.00
$ 90.00	13.50	16.20	18.00
$100.00	15.00	18.00	20.00

Inspecting the Authenticity of Bills

Each bill of U.S. currency has different security features that make the bill difficult to counterfeit. These features also provide ways to determine if bills are authentic. When a customer presents cash, it is important to check the authenticity of the bills, especially when larger denominations are used. Counterfeiters do not often go to great lengths to recreate bills that have little value, such as $1 bills. Also, accepting a large bill that might be counterfeit puts the operation at risk of losing a significant amount of money.

All U.S. currency has a portrait of an historical U.S. figure on the face of the bill. The universal seal to the left of each portrait represents the entire Federal Reserve System. Each bill also has a unique serial number (made up of letters and numbers) printed twice on the front of the note. A letter and number beneath the left serial number identify the issuing Federal Reserve Bank. In addition, features such as watermarks, colored threads, and color-changing ink that reacts to different types of light can make a fake bill lacking these traits easy to spot.

Exhibit 1c on the following pages lists the security features the U.S. Treasury has incorporated on each bill and includes simple ways for you and your staff to check bills for authenticity.

Exhibit 1c

U.S. Paper Currency Security Features

FIVE DOLLAR BILL $5

Portrait: Abraham Lincoln

Security thread: To the left of Lincoln's head; visible when the bill is held up to the light; also glows *blue* when placed under ultraviolet (or black) light.

Microscopic print: "FIVE DOLLARS" appears along the side borders on the front of the bill. "THE UNITED STATES OF AMERICA" appears on the lower edge of the portrait frame.

Watermark: Within the space to the right of the portrait, there is a watermark that looks like the portrait of Abraham Lincoln. It can be seen from both sides by holding the bill up to light.

Additional features: Thin parallel lines printed in the background of the picture on both sides of the bill. These lines appear distorted or splotchy when photocopied.

TEN DOLLAR BILL $10

Portrait: Alexander Hamilton

Security thread: To the right of Hamilton's head; visible when the bill is held up to the light; also glows *orange* when placed under ultraviolet (or black) light.

Microscopic print: "TEN" appears within the "10" on the lower left-hand corner on the front of the bill. "THE UNITED STATES OF AMERICA" appears above Hamilton's name.

Watermark: Within the space to the right of the portrait, there is a watermark that looks like the portrait of Alexander Hamilton. It can be seen from both sides by holding the bill up to light.

Additional features: Thin parallel lines printed in the background of the picture on both sides of the bill. These lines appear distorted or splotchy when photocopied. The number "10" on the lower right-hand corner on the front of the bill changes from green to black when the bill is tilted.

TWENTY DOLLAR BILL $20

Portrait: Andrew Jackson

Security thread: To the left of Jackson's head; visible when the bill is held up to the light; also glows *green* when placed under ultraviolet (or black) light.

Microscopic print: "USA 20" appears within the "20" on the lower left-hand corner on the front of the bill. "THE UNITED STATES OF AMERICA" appears along the lower portion of the portrait frame.

The redesigned $20 note also features additional microprinting on its face: bordering the first three letters of the "TWENTY USA" ribbon to the right of the portrait, the inscription "USA 20" is printed in blue, and "THE UNITED STATES OF AMERICA 20 USA 20" appears in black on the border below the Treasurer's signature.

Watermark: Within the space to the right of the portrait, there is a watermark that looks like the portrait of Andrew Jackson. It can be seen from both sides by holding the bill up to light.

Additional features: Thin parallel lines printed in the background of the picture on both sides of the bill. These lines appear distorted or splotchy when photocopied. The number "20" on the lower right-hand corner on the front of the bill changes from green to black when the bill is tilted.

FIFTY DOLLAR BILL $50

Portrait: Ulysses S. Grant

Security thread: To the right of Grant's head; visible when the bill is held up to the light; also glows *yellow* when placed under ultraviolet (or black) light.

Microscopic print: "FIFTY" is repeated in microscopic print along the side borders on the front of the bill. "THE UNITED STATES OF AMERICA" appears on Grant's collar.

The redesigned $50 note also features additional microprinting on its face: "FIFTY," "USA," and the numeral "50" can be found in two of the blue stars to the left of the portrait.

Watermark: Within the space to the right of the portrait, there is a watermark that looks like the portrait of Ulysses S. Grant. It can be seen from both sides by holding the bill up to light.

Additional features: Thin parallel lines printed in the background of the picture on both sides of the bill. These lines appear distorted or splotchy when photocopied. The number "50" on the lower right-hand corner on the front of the bill changes from green to black when the bill is tilted. Color-shifting ink changes from copper to green when you tilt the note up and down. Also, small yellow "50s" have been printed in the background on the back of the note.

ONE HUNDRED DOLLAR BILL $100

Portrait: Benjamin Franklin

Security thread: To the left of Franklin's head; visible when the bill is held up to the light; also glows *red* when placed under ultraviolet (or black) light.

Microscopic print: "USA 100" is repeated in microscopic print within the 100 on the lower left-hand corner on the front of the bill. "THE UNITED STATES OF AMERICA" appears on Franklin's coat.

Watermark: Within the space to the right of the portrait, there is a watermark that looks like the portrait of Benjamin Franklin. It can be seen from both sides by holding the bill up to light.

Additional Features: Thin parallel lines printed in the background of the picture on both sides of the bill. These lines appear distorted or splotchy when photocopied. The number "100" on the lower right-hand corner on the front of the bill changes from green to black when the bill is tilted.

Counting Back Change

Due to the busy pace and sometimes crowded register area, foodservice employees can easily become distracted when making change. Some con artists, known as "quick-change artists," try to use this to their advantage by claiming they presented a bill of a higher denomination than they actually did. So how does an operation protect itself from such a scam? When making change, it is important for cashiers to follow these steps:

1 **Announce the total owed by the guest.** You should always do this before accepting the customer's payment. "That will be three dollars and eleven cents, please."

2 **When the guest hands over money for payment, place it in a visible spot.** Possible locations include the counter, to the side of the register, or on top of the register.

3 **Announce the value of the payment presented.** "From twenty dollars…"

4 **Verbally count the change upward, from the smallest coin to the largest denomination.** In this example, you will begin making change with four pennies, stating, "4 cents makes 3.15." You will continue to state each denomination and value, adding up to the original amount presented for payment.

5 **Place the change directly into the guest's hand.** Do not leave it on the counter to be picked up.

6 **Once the guest has acknowledged the change, place the original payment into the cash register.** This avoids any confusion on either end or a dispute over how much cash the guest presented.

Change should always be given in the largest denominations possible. For example, it is better to give one dime than two nickels, one quarter instead of two dimes and one nickel, or one five-dollar bill instead of five singles. This can save time and improve accuracy—reducing the likelihood of counting errors.

Activity

Change Is Good

Complete the table below by calculating the correct change amount for each transaction. Then, list the preferred denominations in which the change should be returned to the customer.

Check Total	Cash Presented	Change Amount	Change Denominations
$14.79	Two $10 bills		
$28.45	Three $10 bills		
$42.12	One $50 bill		
$61.70	One $50 bill and one $20 bill		
$65.89	Four $20 bills		

Processing Noncash Payment

Many times a customer will pay with something other than cash. Forms of noncash payment include traveler's checks, personal checks, credit cards, and gift certificates. Depending on the operation, some of these might not be accepted forms of payment.

Traveler's Checks

Traveler's checks are considered the same as cash, and are therefore the target of counterfeiters. Change for a traveler's check is given in actual currency. Traveler's checks come in similar denominations as cash and have security features similar to those found on paper currency. These features include watermarks, raised textures or engraving, and holographic threads.

The most important security feature on traveler's checks is the actual witnessing of the countersigning process itself. When accepting a traveler's check, the owner of the check countersigns the check in the presence of the cashier accepting the check. Then, the signature is compared to the original signature placed on the check at the time of issue. In the case that the check is already countersigned, the presenter should be asked to sign it again on the reverse side and also to present photo identification. The identification should then be compared against the information and signatures on the check.

Indications that a traveler's check has been stolen or had the original signature removed by chemical means (called "washing") include a brownish signature area or missing or smudged background printing. If there are any questions or doubts about accepting a traveler's check, the issuer's customer service department should be contacted for verification of the check.

Personal Checks

Despite the numerous electronic payment options now available (debit cards, credit cards, gift cards, etc.), personal checks are still a popular way of making payments in the United States. However, many foodservice operations do not accept personal checks because of the risks involved. Check fraud is the largest reported fraud in the United States, involving billions of dollars. For check payments, it is standard to ask the customer for proof of identification. Acceptable identification is a valid driver's license or passport—not student or work IDs.

Credit Cards

Credit card machines vary, but their procedures for use are fairly standard. Credit cards are swiped through these machines to obtain authorization from a databank. Then, an authorization response is displayed on the credit card machine. Appropriate actions for each of the specific responses are outlined in *Exhibit 1d*.

Once the credit card has been authorized and the slip has printed out, the customer should total and sign the slip while the cashier keeps the credit card in his or her possession. Before returning the credit card to the customer, the signature on the credit card should be compared with the signature on the credit card slip. This is one way to verify the customer's identity. If the signatures are different, you should politely ask the customer to provide additional identification. Acceptable forms of identification include a valid driver's license or passport.

Typically, credit card payments do not require additional identification unless fraud is suspected or the back of the card has not been signed. One way to detect fraud is to compare the embossed number on the card against the four digits of the account number displayed on the terminal.

After confirming the customer's identity (via signature or other identification), it is then time to return the credit card to the customer along with a copy of the credit card slip.

Exhibit 1d

Credit Card Response and Action Guide

Response	Action
Approved	Ask the customer to sign the sales receipt.
Declined	Return the card to the customer and ask for another card.
Call or Call Center	Call your voice authorization center and tell the operator that you are responding to a "Call" or "Call Center" message. Follow the operator's instructions.
	Note: *In most cases, a "Call" or "Call Center" message just means the card issuer needs some additional information before the transaction can be approved.*
Pick Up	Keep the card if you can do so peacefully.
No Match	Swipe the card and rekey the last four digits. If the "No Match" response appears again, keep the card if you can do so peacefully.

Processing Payment Tableside

The procedure for processing payment as part of table service is very similar to how it is processed at the register. There are four simple steps to process a payment when serving customers tableside.

1 Present the check at the table.

2 Collect payment from the customers.

3 Process payment.

4 Return change or credit card receipt and credit card.

For credit card payments, the card and credit card receipt are brought to the table together. It is helpful for servers to explain to customers which copy they should take. After the customer has left, the signed receipt should be collected and secured immediately.

When processing a cash payment, you do not need to count out the change to the customer and repeat the totals. Simply make change away from the table and then return the change to the customer.

Storing Cash Securely

Loss or theft can happen in the blink of an eye. Once payments have been accepted, receipts must be stored securely. *Exhibit 1e* outlines standard procedures for ensuring the secure storage of cash and noncash receipts at the operation.

Bleeding a register refers to the process of removing extra cash from the register during restaurant operation to store the cash more securely in a safe. This process can also be referred to as *skimming*. A manager usually bleeds a register at set times or after a busy sales rush. The register is counted and all of the money except for a specified amount is removed. The removed money is then immediately put into a pouch and placed in

---

Exhibit 1e

Safeguarding Cash, Checks, and Receipts

1 During hours of operation, restrict access to coins, currency, checks, and credit card receipts. Each cashier should be assigned his or her own cash drawer. If possible, only one person should have access to a register.

2 All payments should be secured in the register, which should be closed at all times and also locked when unattended.

3 Large bills should immediately be stored in a secure location, such as under the register drawer or in a drop safe near the register.

4 Cash, checks, and credit card receipts should be relocated to a safe or other locked secure place at regular intervals determined by the management or when business is slow. Access to the safe should be limited to a minimum number of people. If multiple managers are on during a shift, only one should have access to the safe.

5 When servers end their shifts, the manager should count the money and any credit card receipts and immediately secure them.

6 Money in the safe should be stored in counted-out register drawers or in durable pouches. The zippered pouches keep money and coins secure and are easy to transfer when making deposits.

the safe. A signed slip of paper that reports how much money was taken out is put into the register. Sometimes a manager will quickly skim only for the large bills, such as $50s and $100s, pulling them into a more secure location for storage.

Cash Register Reconciliation

Reconciliation means to check one against another for accuracy. When performing a cash register reconciliation, a comparison is made to confirm that the money, checks, and credit card receipts in the register are equal to the recorded sales for a particular time period (less the amount of the opening cash bank initially in the drawer).

If a manager is not actually conducting the reconciliation, he or she should certainly be overseeing it. Once the money has been turned over to the manager, he or she should always recount it.

Step 1: Run Sales Reports

The first step to performing a cash register reconciliation is to run a sales report. Depending on the restaurant, sales reports should be based on either an individual employee or a specific register. In a counter-service operation, it is common to run sales reports by register. It is better to allow only one employee access to that register during a shift. That way, if there is a discrepancy, you will know who to ask about it. Newer POS/register systems have many security options that prevent anyone except the logged-in cashier to access the cash drawer.

Most table-service restaurants have the servers manage their own money and change during a shift and then print out a sales report at the end of the shift. In this case, a sales report must be run for each server because each one has individual sales records.

Step 2: Count Actual Receipts

Once the sales report is printed, it is time to count the money. When counting a cash register drawer, it is helpful to have a worksheet with a blank table to complete, which separates each bill or coin and has an area for check and credit card totals. It is important to make sure all of the credit card tips have been entered correctly and that you have a signed receipt from each individual credit card transaction.

It is a good policy to always have two people count the contents of the register drawer in each other's presence and/or in view of the video surveillance camera. Once they have agreed to the counted amount, both employees then sign a slip so there is a record of the reconciliation. (See *Exhibit 1f.*)

Exhibit 1f

Two people should count the contents of the register drawer in each other's presence.

Step 3: Identify and Evaluate Variances

Once the register contents have been totaled, the amounts must be compared to the figures on the sales report. If there are any differences—or variances—between the report and the actual count, it is imperative to identify how these variances might have occurred. The solution could simply be that two bills or credit card receipts have stuck together, causing one to go uncounted in the total.

Unfortunately, sometimes the answer is that an employee is stealing from the drawer, or is not able to handle cash properly. Theft or the mishandling of cash, either by employees or by customers, is a very real risk in the restaurant industry. Recording variances is a good way to look for patterns over time. If an employee's drawer is frequently short, he or she should be closely observed and coached.

Overages in a drawer can also be a problem. While they might seem like extra income for the restaurant, they are usually a sign that something careless or tricky is going on. An employee might be overcharging customers and then pocketing the "extra" money. Frequent overages should signal closer observation just as much as frequent shortages should. Any overages should be recorded and the money retained by the restaurant.

Employees should be aware of what will happen if the drawer is over or short at the time of reconciliation. Depending on the operation, employees might be responsible for all shortages. This will keep them on their toes about giving correct change and looking out for customer theft. On the flip side, this can also decrease employee morale. Another practice is to set a certain dollar value that the drawer can be over or short. Whatever over/short policy is implemented, employees should be fully aware of the policy, and it should be followed consistently with each incident.

At the time of reconciliation, all paperwork should be completed promptly. Tax and tip records should be entered into the appropriate reports and variances should be recorded to the appropriate employee.

Preparing Bank Deposits

Preparing a bank deposit is the final step before removing money from the operation. Bank deposits should be made on a daily basis, and sometimes even more than once per day depending on volume. It is not safe, for neither person nor property, to keep large amounts of cash in the operation for any length of time.

Step 1: Count the Deposit

The first step to preparing a bank deposit is to count the cash and traveler's check receipts to determine the amount to be deposited. Every time the contents of the safe are counted, there should be a signed record of how much was removed. Two different people should verify these amounts. The only money left in the safe after a deposit has been made should be petty cash. This amount will vary per restaurant. Petty cash is used in case of emergency and to provide a change bank for the cash register.

Step 2: Prepare the Deposit Slip

Once the total deposit has been counted and confirmed by two people, a deposit slip needs to be prepared. Most banks provide preprinted slips for the convenience of their customers. An example of a bank deposit slip is shown in *Exhibit 1g*. The amount of individual bills and coins should be recorded in the appropriate spaces on the slip. In addition, each check should be listed by its check number and amount. The deposit slip should then be totaled and double-checked by a second person.

Exhibit 1g

FIRST WORLD BANK
545 MAIN STREET
ANYTOWN, USA 54321

THE BURGER STOP
30 Third Avenue
Anytown, USA 54321

ACCOUNT 54976 3154 02

NAME _John Smith_

SIGNATURE _John Smith_

DATE _06/29/08_

VARIFIED BY _BettyRoth_   DATE 6—29

CASH	AMOUNT	CHECKS	AMOUNT
PENNIES	1.12	(List individually)	
NICKELS	2.00	1	56.25
DIMES	2.30	2	61.75
QUARTERS	5.25	3	43.13
		4	105.62
ONE	26	5	7.33
FIVE	35	6	
TEN	40	7	
TWENTY	120	8	
FIFTY	—	9	
HUNDRED	100	10	
CASH TOTAL	331.67	**CHECK TOTAL**	274.08
TOTAL DEPOSIT			605.75

DEPOSIT TICKET

Sample bank deposit slip

Step 3: Secure and Transport the Deposit

Secure the cash for the deposit in a sturdy and locked pouch. The deposit should then be transported directly to the bank, and the manager should make sure he or she receives a deposit receipt confirming that the deposit was made. The deposit should also be recorded in the back office computer system.

Activity

Shift Change at Turascas

It is 3:00 p.m., the end of the day shift on a busy Saturday at Turascas, a Mexican restaurant across from a mall. The day manager, Enrique, is performing the cash register reconciliation at the bar. Gladys, the new night manager, comes in to get ready for the evening shift. She offers to help Enrique by counting the drawer receipts but suggests they relocate to the business office. On the way through the back of the house, Enrique stops on the back dock to talk to a chef who is leaving for the day. Gladys takes the cash drawer from Enrique and unlocks the office. She begins counting the contents of the drawer. When Enrique enters and offers to help, Gladys hands him a stack of bills and says, "Here—tell me if you get $620.00 for this pile." Given this information, answer the following:

1 List the security breaches that put the cash at risk of being mishandled.

2 What are some things that either Enrique or Gladys did properly?

3 What procedure should Gladys and Enrique follow at this point?

Summary

To properly manage a restaurant, there must be guidelines in place to ensure proper cash handling. Many operations already have their own procedures in place, and it is a manager's job to ensure staff are properly trained and procedures enforced.

It is critical to understand what goes into the accurate calculation of guest checks, including subtotals, sales tax, and gratuity. Tools such as tax tables and tip tables can make calculating by hand a quick process.

Each bill of U.S. currency has different security features that make the bill difficult for counterfeiters to duplicate. These features—such as watermarks, colored thread, and color-changing ink—vary by denomination. They provide a variety of ways to determine if bills are authentic. Change should always be given in the largest denominations possible. This can save time and improve accuracy—reducing the likelihood of counting errors.

Forms of noncash payment include personal checks, credit cards, traveler's checks, and gift certificates. Each of these requires procedures for proper security and approval. Depending on the operation, some of these might not be accepted forms of payment.

Several guidelines should be in place to safeguard cash and receipts. Access to cash should be restricted, and cash should be stored securely at all times. Accurate counting and cash register reconciliation can reveal problems or mistakes.

A comparison is made to confirm that the money, checks, and credit card receipts in the register are equal to the recorded sales for a particular time period. This is called cash register reconciliation. Any variances between the report and the actual count should be noted and evaluated. Employees should be aware of what will happen if the drawer is over or short at the time of reconciliation. Whatever the over/short policy is, it should be followed consistently with each incident.

Preparing a bank deposit is the final step before removing money from the operation. Bank deposits should be made on a daily basis, and sometimes even more than once per day, depending on volume. Every bank deposit should be counted and verified by two people.

Review Your Learning

1 How do secret shoppers help management evaluate how well cash handling practices are followed at the operation?

  A. They attempt to use "quick-change" techniques to short the cashier.

  B. They observe employees' actions and report findings back to management.

  C. They secretly approach other customers, asking them about their experiences at the operation.

  D. They try to leave the operation without paying their bill, just to see if an employee notices.

2 Which is *not true* with regard to subtotals?

  A. The subtotal includes both tax and gratuity.

  B. The subtotal includes both food and beverages.

  C. The subtotal is the basis for the calculation of the tax.

  D. The subtotal is the basis for the calculation of the gratuity.

3 If a customer wants to tip a server eighteen percent, what multiplier would be used to calculate the gratuity?

  A. 0.018   C. 1.18

  B. 0.18   D. 1.80

4 Which of the following is true?

  A. Banks mark random bills to track their routing.

  B. Counterfeiters do not bother to reproduce bills that have a value of $5 or less.

  C. All security features can be spotted with the naked eye in normal daylight conditions.

  D. All U.S. bills have security features that can be checked to verify authenticity.

5 The most critical part of accepting a traveler's check for payment is

  A. verifying the validity of the check with its issuer.

  B. witnessing the countersigning of the traveler's check.

  C. holding the check up to the light to look at the watermark.

  D. asking for valid identification from the person presenting the check.

6 What does it mean to "bleed" the register?

  A. To exchange one person's cash drawer with another's

  B. To prepare the cash for the register reconciliation process

  C. To allow more than one cashier access to the same register

  D. To remove excess cash and large bills to a more secure location

7 What is the purpose of cash register reconciliation?

  A. To compare the contents of the register to the recorded sales for a particular period

  B. To identify variances and possible security breaches related to cash handling

  C. To monitor the performance and accuracy of individual cashiers

  D. All of the above

8 How often should bank deposits be made?

  A. Daily

  B. Weekly

  C. Monthly

  D. Any of the above

Notes

Managing Payables and Receivables

Inside This Chapter

- Accounts Payable
- Accounts Receivable

After completing this chapter, you should be able to:

- Define accounts payable and describe a process for managing them.
- Define accounts receivable and describe a process for managing them.

Key Terms

Account code	Chart of accounts
Accounts payable	Credit terms
Accounts receivable	Invoice
Aging schedule	Voucher

Introduction

As a constant part of business, money is always flowing. Money and goods flow among suppliers and vendors to buyers and customers. A foodservice operation can be both customer and vendor on any given day. For example, a restaurant manager might purchase fruit from a produce supplier in order to sell a fruit salad to a guest.

How can you track all the ins and outs of this flow of money among businesses and customers? It is important to implement a system that makes the recording and processing of such transactions accurate and yet convenient. There are two sides to this tracking system; they are called accounts payable and accounts receivable.

Accounts Payable

Accounts payable is a term used to describe money the operation owes to others, such as suppliers of food, beverages, and other services. Such accounts need to be closely managed and monitored through the use of an established process. Unintentional oversights or theft can easily occur when these accounts are mishandled.

Processing Payments

Every operation should have a system in place to ensure bills are paid in an accurate and consistent manner. Systems for processing payment may differ among operations, but they generally include procedures related to the following four steps:

1. Receive invoices.
2. Code or categorize invoices.
3. Authorize payment of invoices.
4. Pay invoices.

Step 1: Receive Invoices

An **invoice** is a document from a vendor that lists such details as items purchased, date of order, purchaser, and sales price. An invoice is also called a *bill*. Often, invoices also include information such as payment terms or credit and return policies. When a shipment is delivered to the restaurant, an invoice is sometimes included with the delivery. Invoices can also be received from vendors through the mail. Many suppliers simply send bills out on a regular basis, such as monthly or weekly. It is important to compare all invoices to your receiving records to ensure you are being billed accurately.

There should be a designated place to put invoices as they are received at the operation. A bulletin board, or a simple in-box or file folder clearly labeled for invoices only, will help keep invoices from being lost, misplaced, or perhaps overlooked. If, for any reason, a vendor is not paid on time, it will likely affect the operation's ability to get credit in the future. This can make even simple transactions, such as ordering supplies, quite complicated.

Step 2: Code or Categorize Invoices

It is important to categorize payables so that the operation has an accurate, detailed history of its costs of doing business. This cost information aids in the budget planning process and can also indicate where spending has fallen outside of what was expected. These topics related to costs and budgeting will be discussed in detail later in this guide. For now, it is important to know that *keeping accurate cost records is a necessary first step in the overall management of an operation's finances.* Categorizing payables is an important part of that process.

When preparing invoices for payment, they should be coded according to the operation's established chart of accounts. A **chart of accounts** is simply a list of categories used to organize an operation's expense information.

In the foodservice industry, these accounts commonly include categories similar to the following:

- Food
- Beverages
- Supplies (other than food, such as paper products, chemicals)
- Services (exterminator, equipment maintenance, landscaping)
- Advertising
- Utilities

A unique number, or **account code,** is usually assigned to each of the accounts listed on the chart of accounts. These codes might be specific to one operation or department, or might be codes determined by a corporate office. Such codes aid in tracking the costs for the operation.

Here is an example: at the Hotel Bayview, some beverages are ordered separately by the lobby bar, the restaurant, the pool bar, and the banquet departments. The managers for each of these different areas approve invoices for such items that are ordered and received by their departments. The Hotel Bayview has an established code number of "75" for beverages. When an invoice comes in to the pool bar for piña colada mix, the manager of the pool bar will code it to 75 when approving it for payment. The same is true for champagne received in the banquet area, and so forth. If coding is accurate and consistent, when the general manager of the hotel looks at a report for account code 75, it will reflect a summary of all the beverage expenditures for the entire hotel operation.

Step 3: Authorize Payment of Invoices

The accounts payable system should include a step in which payment is actually approved by someone with the authority to do so. This person should be aware of the overall budget for the operation and also be aware of the current state of the operation's finances. Usually, the manager will review the paperwork to ensure it is accurate, and then sign the invoice as approved to be paid. This authorization process can catch errors and also help prevent theft.

Step 4: Pay Invoices

Once all the other steps have been completed, the bill or invoice should be paid in full. It is important to keep a record of the payment, including the check number and date of the payment. The voucher system described in the next section is a good way to record and monitor this process.

Timely payment of accounts payable is also important. Many vendors give discounts for early payments. For example, an invoice might specify something like "2/10, net 30." This indicates that if payment is received by the vendor within ten days of the invoice date, then the operation will get a 2 percent discount on the invoice. The term "net 30" means that the entire bill is due within thirty days—no later. Managers should be aware of these discount opportunities and try to pay bills accordingly to take advantage of those savings whenever possible.

Prompt payment also ensures a good reputation with the supplier. In contrast, once a restaurant has a known history of being delinquent, it may be difficult to obtain food, beverages, supplies, or services on anything other than a cash basis, which could be inconvenient and problematic for the operator.

Activity

Code the Invoice

Jo, the manager of the Dairy Joynt, has received several invoices this week. As she prepares to pay these invoices, she is going to code each one to the appropriate account listed on her chart of accounts. For each vendor listed below, note the account to which its invoice should be coded.

Chart of Accounts			
Code #	Account	Code #	Vendor
30	Food and beverage		**1** Kimball's Paper Products
31	Supplies		**2** Neon Sign Repair Pro
32	Services		**3** Giant Ice
33	Advertising		**4** Cool Breeze Ice Cream Company
34	Utilities		**5** *Main Town Herald* newspaper
			6 Mid-Bay Electric Company
			7 Fresh Farms Produce
			8 Johnson Security Patrols

Using Vouchers

A voucher system is a way to keep records of payments made to vendors. When a manager authorizes payment of an invoice, an accounts payable voucher is then prepared. **Vouchers** are numbered forms that have space to record the information about the payment. This information should include the date of the payment, the check number, and the amount and recipient of the check. An example of an accounts payable voucher is shown in *Exhibit 2a*. The purchase order and signed invoice can also be attached to the voucher to show proof of the actual order and that the order was received.

Exhibit 2a

ACCOUNTS PAYABLE VOUCHER

Voucher #: _XB445_

Prepared by: _____

Approved for payment by: _____

Pay to: _____

Posted by: _____

Address: _____

Audited by: _____

Date paid: _____

Amount of check: _____

Check #: _____

Date	Description	Amount	Discount amount	Net amount	Account code	Amount

Sample accounts payable voucher

Accounts Receivable

Accounts receivable are those amounts due to the operation from others, usually customers and clients. In a restaurant operation, accounts receivable will most likely include house accounts and credit card accounts. Using a system to keep track of accounts receivable is as vital as it is for accounts payable.

House Accounts

Before a manager allows someone to establish a house account at the operation, there should first be a thorough explanation of any credit terms. **Credit terms** are the payment rules established for the account. These include such terms as how much credit is to be extended (credit limit) and when and how often payment is to be received, as well as any fees or penalties for a late payment. If a payment is late, management needs to stick to the agreed-upon credit terms to prevent further late payments. These terms can help prevent huge losses from an individual account.

Think About It...

Why does it matter if clients pay their bills on time or not, as long as the operation eventually gets the money it is owed?

Tracking and Collecting Receivables

Similar to the system for accounts payable, managers need to follow a reliable process to effectively manage accounts receivable. Any accounts receivable system should include the following four steps:

Step 1: Record Receivables Accurately

Any time an item or service has been delivered, it should be immediately recorded. This will ensure accurate billing and minimize the likelihood of forgetting the details of who owes what.

Step 2: Generate Bills and Invoices Promptly

The sooner a bill is generated and delivered to the client, the sooner the clock starts ticking on the window of time for payment. Usually, bills are due thirty days after the date of the invoice, though these terms might vary based on the customer, his or her history with the operation, volume of business, and other factors.

Step 3: Collect Delinquent Accounts Effectively

Money that has not been received after the service has been completed is not earning a return for the operation, thus causing a greater loss than just the amount of the unpaid bill itself. The longer the bill remains uncollected, the more money is lost. Collection procedures typically begin with a series of reminder phone calls. Handled delicately and professionally, many receivables are paid after such contact. Any such contact should be documented. In extreme cases, delinquent accounts might be sent to a lawyer or collection agency for further action.

Using an Aging Schedule

It is helpful for managers to look at an operation's accounts receivable to determine how old the receivables are, or in other words, how long they have remained unpaid. Most operation's credit terms state that receivables more than a certain number of days old are considered past due.

A tool for reviewing such information is called an aging schedule. An **aging schedule** is a chart that shows the "age" of all receivables not yet paid. The schedule reflects the totals for an operation's outstanding accounts receivable, broken down in thirty-day increments. Percentages are assigned to each age category as well. *Exhibit 2b* on the next page shows a sample aging schedule for an operation.

Exhibit 2b

Sample Aging Schedule

Age	January 31, 2008		February 29, 2008	
0–30 Days	$4,000	74.7%	$3,000	50.9%
31–60 Days	1,000	18.7	2,000	33.9
61–90 Days	250	4.7	750	12.7
Over 90 Days	100	1.9	150	2.5
Total	**$5,350**	**100.0%**	**$5,900**	**100.0%**

According to the information in *Exhibit 2b*, at the end of January, about 75 percent of the total outstanding receivables were less than thirty days old. At the end of February, only about 51 percent were that young. Though this might appear positive at first, it is clear that $1,000 moved from the 0–30 days category into the 31–60 days category during that one-month period. When the February receivables older than thirty days are added together, you can see that the amount is about 49 percent of the total outstanding receivables. In January, only about 25 percent of the total receivables were older than thirty days.

Based on this example, it is evident that while this operation did not accrue many new accounts receivable during the month of February, the accounts receivable from prior months are getting older and still have not been paid. This is a good indication that the operation needs to focus more attention on collecting past-due receivables. Depending on the credit terms for the accounts, late fees might be charged to these accounts as well.

Step 4: Record, Store, and Deposit Payments

As discussed in detail in Chapter 1, any payments that have been received should be recorded, stored securely, and deposited as soon as possible. This ensures that accurate records have been taken, and allows the money to start earning a return.

Activity

Mr. Yee and the Green Garden

Damon is the manager of a buffet-style, salad-bar restaurant called Green Garden. One of his regular customers is Mr. Yee, who owns an import business across the street. For years, Mr. Yee has been bringing his business clients to Green Garden for its buffet lunch. It is convenient, and he always knows it will cost $7.95 per client. Mr. Yee has been a customer since before Damon was even hired.

When Damon reviews the accounts receivable for Green Garden, he notices that Mr. Yee's account is more than ninety days past due, which is very out of character. Mr. Yee is still bringing his clients to lunch at least twice a week, but he has not made a payment in over three months. Every visit is still recorded in Mr. Yee's house account and added to his running total. Damon searches, but cannot find a written record of the credit terms of Mr. Yee's house account. Given this information, answer the following:

1 How should Damon approach Mr. Yee about his past-due house account?

_____

_____

_____

_____

_____

_____

_____

2 What are some possible credit terms that Damon might want to establish for Mr. Yee's account? For the short term? For the long term?

_____

_____

_____

_____

_____

_____

_____

Summary

A foodservice operation can be both customer and vendor on any given day. It is important to implement a system that makes the recording and processing of such transactions accurate and yet convenient.

Accounts payable is a term used to describe money the operation owes to others, such as suppliers of food, beverages, and other services. Such accounts need to be closely managed and monitored through the use of an established system. It is important to categorize payables using a chart of accounts so that the operation has an accurate, detailed history of its costs.

There are four basic steps to paying bills in an accurate manner. Every operation should have a system in place that ensures these payment-processing steps are followed consistently. Timely payment of accounts payable is also important, as many vendors give discounts for early payments. Prompt payment also ensures a good reputation with the supplier. A voucher system is one way to keep records of payments made to vendors.

Accounts receivable are those amounts due to the operation from others, usually customers and clients. In a restaurant operation, accounts receivable will most likely include house accounts and credit card accounts. Using a system to keep track of accounts receivable is as vital as it is for accounts payable.

Credit terms are the payment rules established for the account. These include such terms as how much credit is to be extended (credit limit) and when and how often payment is to be received, as well as any fees or penalties for a late payment.

The focus of an accounts receivable system should be to ensure that invoices are mailed out promptly and delinquent accounts are pursued. A good way to look at accounts receivable is to prepare an aging schedule showing the age of the accounts that are past due or outstanding.

Review Your Learning

1 An invoice is also called a

A. bill.

B. credit.

C. voucher.

D. receivable.

2 Which of the following is *not* a part of the accounts payable process?

A. Writing checks

B. Coding invoices

C. Depositing receipts

D. Authorizing payments

3 The tool used to categorize payables is called what?

A. Credit term

B. Aging schedule

C. Voucher system

D. Chart of accounts

4 In a foodservice operation, who is most likely to be accounts receivable?

A. Employees

B. Landscapers

C. Food suppliers

D. Corporate clients

5 An aging schedule shows the

A. amount of receivables past due.

B. customers with the best credit record.

C. customers with the oldest credit history.

D. ages of the customers who have credit accounts.

Notes

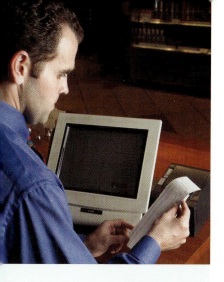

Exploring Costs

Inside This Chapter

- Controllable and Noncontrollable Costs
- Fixed, Variable, and Semivariable Costs
- Crossover of Cost Classifications

After completing this chapter, you should be able to:

- Classify foodservice costs as controllable or noncontrollable.
- Describe and give examples of controllable and noncontrollable costs.
- Classify foodservice costs as variable, semivariable, or fixed.
- Describe and give examples of variable, semivariable, and fixed costs.

1 **True or False:** Hourly employee wages are an example of a noncontrollable cost. *(See p. 33.)*

2 **True or False:** Understanding the different types of costs is key to making effective cost control decisions. *(See p. 32.)*

3 **True or False:** Fixed costs remain the same regardless of sales volume. *(See p. 34.)*

4 **True or False**: A cost can be classified as both fixed and variable. *(See pp. 34–35.)*

5 **True or False:** A cost can be classified as both variable and controllable. *(See pp. 32–35.)*

Key Terms

Controllable cost	Semivariable cost
Fixed cost	Variable cost
Noncontrollable cost	

Introduction

Costs can be classified in several different ways. Cost categorization is used when preparing budgets, forecasts, and figuring break-even points. In the foodservice industry, the most common classifications are controllable and noncontrollable costs, as well as fixed, variable, and semivariable costs. The reason for classifying costs is to differentiate between those costs that management can control and those over which management has little or no control. Identifying and understanding these different types of costs help managers interpret cost-related information and make financial decisions.

Controllable and Noncontrollable Costs

One method of classifying costs is to categorize them as either controllable costs or noncontrollable costs. These are exactly what their names imply. **Controllable costs** are those costs that management can directly control. **Noncontrollable costs** are those costs over which management has little or no control.

Think About It...

Why would a manager need to identify which costs are controllable and which are noncontrollable?

Controllable Costs

An example of a controllable cost is food cost. Management can control this cost by using standardized recipes or exercising standard procedures for portion control, menu listing, and pricing, or by one of several other restraints. For example, if the price of chicken increases and no action is taken, the restaurant's food cost will increase. At this point, management can either raise the selling price of all chicken entrées, reduce portions, reposition the items on the menu, or eliminate chicken from the menu altogether. By taking action, management has controlled the effect of the increased cost of chicken, resulting in no increase in the restaurant's food cost.

Another example of a controllable cost is labor cost. By changing the number of hours worked on an employee's schedule, a manager can affect labor costs. For example, if a restaurant's sales drop, and no action is taken, payroll cost as a percentage of sales increases. By reducing the number of hours worked by employees, this percentage could be brought back into line.

It should be pointed out, however, that in exercising these options, management must always be careful not to alienate customers. If the selling price of chicken entrées is increased too much, or too many hours are trimmed off the schedule, resulting in poor service, customers could be driven to the competition.

Noncontrollable Costs

An example of a noncontrollable cost is insurance. Once an insurance policy has been negotiated, management has no control over the cost of that policy. Another example is license fees. Management has no control over the rate charged for bar or occupation licenses. A third example is the operation's lease or mortgage. Once signed, management has virtually no control over this cost.

Activity

Classify the Cost

Classify each cost listed as either *controllable* (c) or *noncontrollable* (n).

_____ **1** Electricity　　_____ **3** Beverages　　_____ **5** Rent

_____ **2** Wages　　_____ **4** Insurance　　_____ **6** Food

Activity

Cost Cutting Practice

Julia is reviewing a list of expenses for the operation of her restaurant. She notices several jumps in costs compared to the previous month. The items that have increased in cost are:

- Electricity
- Gas
- Produce delivery fees
- Milk

Given this information, answer the following:

1 What can Julia do to reduce any of these costs in the upcoming months?

_____

_____

2 How might these changes affect the restaurant's customers?

_____

_____

3 Are there any costs that Julia could not really reduce?

_____

_____

Fixed, Variable, and Semivariable Costs

In addition to being classified as either controllable or noncontrollable, costs can also be expressed as fixed, variable, or semivariable. This group of classifications is based on each cost's relationship to sales volume. In other words, does a cost increase or decrease as sales increase or decrease?

Fixed costs

Fixed costs are those costs that remain the same regardless of sales volume. Insurance is an example of a fixed cost. As previously mentioned, once the insurance policies have been negotiated, the cost remains the same throughout the term of the policy. For example, if the cost of insuring the business is $1,000 per month, it will remain at $1,000 every month. If the restaurant has sales of $10,000 one month, $20,000 the next month, and $15,000 the following month, the insurance cost remains the same for each month at $1,000. It would not change because sales levels have changed.

Variable Costs

Variable costs are those costs that go up and down as sales go up and down and do so in direct proportion. An example of a variable cost is food cost. As sales go up, more food is purchased to replenish inventory, and as sales go down, less food is purchased. If adequate controls are in place and there is little waste or theft, the amount of food used is in direct proportion to sales.

Semivariable Costs

Semivariable costs go up and down as sales go up and down, but not in direct proportion. Semivariable costs are made up of both fixed costs and variable costs. An example of a semivariable cost is labor. Management is normally paid a salary. The salary remains the same regardless of the operation's sales volume. If the general manager, assistant manager, and chef are collectively paid $160,000 per year, they will receive that amount regardless of whether the restaurant brings in $1,000,000 or $1,300,000 per year. Thus, management's salary is a fixed cost. That is, it remains the same regardless of volume.

On the other hand, staff members such as the wait staff and line cooks are paid an hourly wage and are scheduled according to anticipated sales. As a result, the cost of hourly employees goes up as sales go up and goes down as sales go down. (See *Exhibit 3a*.) If proper scheduling is used, the cost will go up and down in direct proportion to sales levels. Putting this all together, labor is considered a semivariable cost because there is a fixed cost component (management's salary) and a variable cost component (hourly staff wages).

Exhibit 3a

Labor is considered a semivariable cost because it has a fixed component (salaried employees), as well as a variable component (hourly employees).

Activity

How Variable Is the Cost?

Classify each cost listed as either *fixed* (f), *variable* (v), or *semivariable* (s).

_____ **1** Electricity   _____ **3** Beverages   _____ **5** Rent

_____ **2** Wages   _____ **4** Insurance   _____ **6** Food

Crossover of Cost Classifications

Clearly, there is some crossover in classifying costs. Variable and semivariable costs are usually controllable costs. Fixed costs are typically noncontrollable costs. While there are some exceptions to this, for the most part it is true.

Another thing to consider is that a particular cost could be classified differently depending on how it is budgeted. For example, if a restaurant's lease is negotiated at $3,000 per month, rent is then a fixed cost. It does not vary according to sales, neither increasing as sales go up nor decreasing as sales go down. It will always be the same at $3,000. If, on the other hand, the lease is negotiated at 6 percent of sales, rent is then a variable cost. The dollar amount will go up as sales go up and down as sales go down, doing so in direct proportion.

Another possibility is that the lease calls for a monthly payment of $1,000 plus 3 percent of sales. Then rent is a semivariable cost. The $1,000 is paid regardless of sales volume, making it a fixed cost. The variable part of the cost comes from the 3 percent of sales, which increases or decreases as sales go up or down in direct proportion. As discussed earlier, a cost with both fixed and variable attributes is a semivariable cost. It goes up and down as sales go up and down, but not in direct proportion.

From this example it can be seen that some costs, depending on how they are structured, can be classified as either fixed, variable, or semivariable. This is also a good example of the exception to the rule stated previously that variable and semivariable costs are normally controllable. In this case, these costs are noncontrollable because the lease cannot be changed until it expires; thus management has no control over the lease payment.

Think About It...

How might the way a cost is budgeted affect how it is categorized?

Another example is advertising. If management determines that they will spend two percent of sales on advertising, it is then a variable cost. It will go up and down in direct proportion to sales. If, on the other hand, they decide to spend $2,500 per month on advertising, it is then a fixed cost. It will not change as sales volume changes.

Summary

Costs can be classified in several ways. Cost categorization is used when preparing budgets, forecasting, and figuring break-even points.

One method of classifying costs in the foodservice industry is to categorize them as either controllable or noncontrollable costs. These are exactly what their names imply. Controllable costs are those costs that management can directly control. Examples include food cost and labor cost. Noncontrollable costs are those costs over which management has little or no control. Examples include insurance and license fees.

In addition to controllable and noncontrollable, costs can also be expressed as either fixed, variable, or semivariable. This group of classifications is based on each cost's relationship to sales volume. Fixed costs remain the same regardless of sales volume. Insurance is an example. Variable costs go up and down as sales go up and down, and do so in direct proportion. An example is food cost. Semivariable costs are made up of both fixed costs and variable costs. An example of this is labor.

Some crossover is expected in classifying costs. Variable and semivariable costs are usually controllable. Fixed costs are typically noncontrollable. While there are some exceptions to this, for the most part it is true. Also, a particular cost can be classified differently depending on how it is budgeted.

Review Your Learning

1 Which is an example of a controllable cost?

   A. Labor

   B. License fees

   C. Insurance

   D. Property tax

2 Which is an example of a noncontrollable cost?

   A. Rent

   B. Food

   C. Advertising

   D. Hourly wages

3 A noncontrollable cost

   A. is repeatedly negotiated.

   B. is usually a fixed cost.

   C. is considered a high-risk cost.

   D. does not change as sales volume changes.

4 Which is *true* related to fixed costs?

   A. Management generally can control fixed costs.

   B. Once they are negotiated, fixed costs remain the same.

   C. Fixed costs change as sales volume increases or decreases.

   D. Fixed costs can have both a fixed component and a variable component.

5 Which is an example of a variable cost?

   A. Mortgage

   B. Insurance

   C. Landscaping

   D. Hourly wages

6 Which is an example of a semivariable cost?

   A. Food

   B. Labor

   C. Insurance

   D. Electricity

Preparing the Operating Budget

4

Inside This Chapter

- What Is an Operating Budget?
- Forecasting Sales Revenue
- Forecasting Costs
- Putting It All Together

After completing this chapter, you should be able to:

- Describe a foodservice operating budget.
- Forecast foodservice sales revenues and guest counts.
- Forecast foodservice operating costs.
- Prepare a master labor schedule for a foodservice operation.

Test Your Knowledge

1 **True or False:** Operating budgets can be used to outline a manager's performance goals. *(See p. 41.)*

2 **True or False:** The operating budget for a foodservice operation includes forecasts for both expenses and revenues. *(See p. 40.)*

3 **True or False:** An accurate operating budget can be prepared without any historical information for the operation. *(See p. 41.)*

4 **True or False:** The two major costs in a foodservice operation are food and utilities. *(See p. 42.)*

5 **True or False:** It is a good idea to always schedule a few more cooks and servers than you think you will need. *(See p. 45.)*

Key Terms

Covers per server

Depreciation

Food cost

Food cost percentage

Forecast

Master schedule

Moving average

Operating budget

Standard

Introduction

When it comes to finances, it is easy to spend more than intended. Having a budget helps managers plan the financial activity related to their daily operations. A budget serves as a guide for making appropriate spending decisions, both in the short and long term. While a budget can be an important valuable tool, it is important to note that a budget is only as accurate as the care and detail that go into its preparation.

What Is an Operating Budget?

An **operating budget** is a projected financial plan for a specific period of time. It lists the anticipated sales revenue and projected expenses and gives an estimate of the profit or loss for the period. Operating budgets are often prepared monthly, though they can be prepared for shorter or longer periods depending on the structure of the organization. Operating budgets serve many purposes in the management of a foodservice operation.

These include:

- Analyzing needs, such as staffing, food, and supplies
- Outlining operating goals and managers' performance responsibilities
- Measuring actual performance against anticipated performance

While an operating budget is a necessary tool for foodservice managers, preparing one is not a simple process. Putting together a useful and accurate budget requires time and care.

Forecasting Sales Revenue

Most operating budgets are based on forecasts. A **forecast** is a prediction of sales levels or costs that will occur during a specific time period. A variety of methods are used to forecast foodservice sales and costs, and most of them rely directly on having accurate historical data for the operation. To plan for the future, you must look at what has occurred in the past. Intuition and experience have important roles in the forecasting process as well.

The first step in creating an operating budget is forecasting anticipated sales revenue for the operation. This figure will affect many other items to be included in the budget. As discussed in the previous chapter, some costs change as sales levels fluctuate. That is why it is especially important to start with a solid sales forecast before calculating any other figures of the operating budget.

Sales levels are almost always based on the number of customers and average sales per customer. The most common food service revenue forecasting techniques are based on the following calculation:

$$\text{Number of customers} \times \text{Average sales per customer} = \text{Sales forecast}$$

So, how does a manager determine the figures to use in this calculation? Operational records, such as sales histories and production sheets, provide this valuable historical information. (*See Exhibit 4a.*) These

Exhibit 4a

Day and Date: Tuesday, July 1
Weather: Sunny
Total Meals Served: 200

Meal: Dinner

Item	Forecasted	Prepared	Number Sold	Waste
Salmon	45	45	40	5
Beef Filet	30	25	22	3
Baked Ham	70	70	61	2
Lasagna	80	75	67	8
Lamb Chop	5	10	10	0
	230	225	200	18

Sample production sheet

records, when carefully analyzed, can be used to calculate what has happened in the past, including trends related to menu item popularity.

There are several software products available to calculate sales forecasts. Most operations can run historical sales and production reports from their point-of-sale (POS) systems. The information on these reports is then used to anticipate what is likely to occur moving forward.

Many forecasting methods assume that what happened last week will happen this week, which is not always accurate. An operation can have good sales weeks followed by bad sales weeks due to factors beyond management's control. Severe weather, road construction, or other events can drastically affect sales levels. It is misleading to assume that a period's sales forecast will be exactly the same as the previous period's actual sales.

One way to forecast in spite of such fluctuations is to use the **moving average** technique. Using this technique, sales information for two or three recent and similar periods is averaged together. The average can produce a forecast that is more likely to be accurate, since it is not based solely on one period that might have had unique circumstances.

Forecasting Costs

Once there is a reliable forecast of sales revenue, management can move forward and forecast costs for the budget period. Because past history is key to accurate cost forecasting, managers should use any available records and tools to analyze historical cost data.

In general, the three categories of costs for a foodservice operation are:

1. Food costs
2. Labor costs
3. Other costs

Food costs and labor costs each have components that are directly related to sales levels and are therefore considered to be either variable or semivariable costs. Because of this relationship, it is easy to see why accurate sales information is vitally important to consider in managers' forecasts. Additionally, there are other costs, which include items such as utilities, marketing, and equipment maintenance. These costs are often refered to as "overhead".

Activity

Fantastic Egg Forecast

Fantastic Egg is a breakfast-only restaurant with an average sales price of $4.25 per customer. The restaurant is open from 6:00 a.m. to 1:00 p.m., Wednesday through Sunday, and is closed on Monday and Tuesday. The restaurant averages 175 customers per day on weekdays and 240 per day on weekend days.

1 What is the sales forecast for an average week? _____

Now, assume the Thanksgiving holiday is occurring in the upcoming week. Fantastic Egg will not open on Thanksgiving Day, but it is open the day after Thanksgiving. The average customer count for the day after Thanksgiving is usually double that of an average weekend day. This is due to the large groups of early-bird holiday shoppers out that morning.

2 What is the forecasted sales for the week of Thanksgiving? _____

Food Costs

Food cost is the actual dollar value of the food used during a certain period. The key to forecasting food cost is to know the desired, or target, food cost percentage. Food cost percentage is a measurement of the relationship between sales and the expense spent on food in order to generate those sales.

Food cost is forecast using the following formula:

Sales forecast × Food cost percentage = Food cost forecast

For example, if a restaurant's forecasted sales are $14,500 for a period, and the standard food cost percentage for the operation is 27 percent, then the forecasted food cost is $3,915.

$14,500 × .27 = $3,915

As long as management has a sales forecast and a target food cost percentage, the calculation of the forecasted food cost is very straightforward. The concepts of food cost and food cost percentage will be explored in further detail in Chapter 6.

Labor Costs

Anticipated labor costs can be complicated to calculate. Fortunately, there is a step-by-step process that managers can follow to forecast these costs for their operations.

Think About It...

Inaccurate sales forecasts could cause either too many employees being scheduled or too much food being purchased, resulting in lost profit to the restaurant. If not enough employees are scheduled or not enough food is purchased, it could result in poor customer service as well as the possibility of running out of popular menu items. How could these conditions affect sales for the period? How could they affect long-term sales?

Step 1: Total Available Labor Dollars

Figuring the amount that can be spent on labor is often tied to a standard. A **standard** is what a cost should be. Standards are determined by management and are designed so an operation can achieve a profit. Like food cost, labor cost is usually given a standard that is expressed as a percentage. (Again, the calculations to determine labor cost percentage will be explored in detail in Chapter 6.)

To determine the total available labor dollars for a period, the standard labor cost percentage is multiplied by the Sales forecast for the period.

$$\text{Standard labor cost percentage} \times \text{Sales forecast} = \text{\$ available for labor}$$

For example, if the standard labor cost percentage for the Tiki Hut is 28 percent, and the sales forecast for next week is $17,000, the amount of money available for labor for that week is $4,760.

$4,760 × $17,000 = .28 or 28%

Step 2: Subtract Costs of Benefits and Deductions

Now that there is a forecasted amount of money available for labor, the next step is to subtract the cost of benefits and deductions. These amounts must be accounted for and subtracted from the total dollars available for labor.

Suppose the Tiki Hut expects to spend $1,748 on benefits and standard deductions during the upcoming one-week period. The dollars available for payroll would now look like this:

> **$4,760 available for labor**
>
> **− $1,748 benefits and deductions**
> _____
>
> **= $3,012 remaining payroll available**

Step 3: Subtract Fixed Labor Costs

Now that the dollar amount available for scheduling employees has been calculated, the next step is to figure how much of payroll is a fixed cost (management salaries) and how much is variable (hourly employees). This is important for creating a work schedule because, for the most part, only the variable cost employees are listed.

To figure how many dollars are available for scheduling hourly employees, subtract the total of fixed-cost (management) salaries from the payroll dollars available.

Payroll dollars available	−	Fixed-cost salaries	=	Dollars available for variable employees

Assume that management salaries at the Tiki Hut total $1,350 per week. The labor dollars are available for hourly employees are then $1,662.

$3,012 − $1,350 = $1,662

Step 4: Distribute Remaining Labor Dollars Among Hourly Positions

Once the amount that can be spent on hourly employees is known, it must be broken down between the front-of-the-house and back-of-the-house positions. The reason for this is the difference in hourly wages paid to these employees. Servers generally receive tips and are therefore paid less by the restaurant than job classifications that do not receive tips.

You can determine the hourly staff needed by using productivity standards. The most efficient method of scheduling the service staff is by using a labor productivity standard known as covers per server. **Covers per server** are the number of customer meals that a waitstaff member can serve in an hour. Each operation should have a standard figure for covers per server that is based on past customer counts and productivity levels. This standard is then measured against the sales forecast to determine the number of servers to schedule.

At the Tiki Hut, the production standard is twenty covers per server per hour. The forecast for a daily lunch rush (assuming a four-hour period) is three hundred covers. Using this information, 3.75 servers must be scheduled.

300 covers ÷ 4 hours = 75 covers per hour

75 covers per hour ÷ 20 covers per server = 3.75 servers

The number of servers to schedule is rarely even. The question then becomes: round up or round down? There is no static answer, as it depends on the employees involved. If the staff is relatively new and not fully trained, it would be wise to round up and add another person. On the other hand, if the staff is experienced with a high productivity ratio, it would probably be best to drop a person.

The service schedule should then be further refined, as not all of the guests are going to arrive in an orderly fashion of seventy-five guests per hour. In the example shown in *Exhibit 4b* on the next page, during the hour of 12:00–1:00 p.m., a spike of ninety covers is

Exhibit 4b

Standard Service Schedule for the Tiki Hut

Position	10:00	11:00	12:00	1:00	2:00	Total
Total covers	15	75	80	90	40	**300**
Server A						5 hours
Server B						4 hours
Server C						3 hours
Server D						3 hours
Total hours						**15 hours**

expected, which is ten covers more than the standard for the four servers. During this time period, the wait staff will be working at a maximum rate with four servers. Consequently, the schedule may call for one server to open and then more servers can be added as the customer count increases over the meal period. Given these patterns, the schedule would look something similar to that shown in *Exhibit 4b*.

Once the servers are scheduled, the number of hours available for the rest of the positions needs to be determined. How does management know what amount is left to work with? Determining the remaining payroll dollars available is calculated using the following formula:

$$\text{Payroll dollars available} - \text{Fixed payroll dollars} - \text{Server payroll dollars} = \text{Remaining payroll dollars available}$$

At the Tiki Hut, four servers have been scheduled for the time period of 10:00 a.m. to 2:00 p.m. You can see in *Exhibit 4b* that the total hours for servers for that shift are fifteen. Assuming a rate of $2.13 per hour, the server payroll for the day is $31.95. Assuming the restaurant is open six days, the server payroll for the week is $191.70. Look at the remaining payroll dollars available for the other hourly positions at the Tiki Hut:

$3,212 − $1,350 − $192 = $1,670

At this point, the remaining payroll dollars available is divided by the average wage per hour to determine the number of hours available to schedule. Again, each operation should have a standard figure used as its average wage per hour. Keep in mind that this standard is an average and some employees will make more than this and some will make less. (The calculations to determine average wage per hour will be in detail explained in Chapter 6.)

$$\text{Remaining payroll dollars available} \div \text{Average wage per hour} = \text{Number of hours available to schedule remaining hourly employees}$$

The resulting number gives the manager a good idea of how many hours are left to work with. Assuming the average hourly rate per hour at the Tiki Hut is $7.50, the number of hours

A master schedule is not absolute. It is created with the idea that this sales level is what is most often likely to occur. Therefore, a master schedule is considered a norm. As sales change from the norm, the master schedule is adjusted accordingly.

remaining available to schedule hourly employees for the week can be determined.

$$\$1,670 \div \$7.50 = 223 \text{ hours}$$

Step 5: Complete the Master Schedule

Creating a good work schedule for a restaurant is difficult, but not impossible. The right number of reliable people with the right combination of experience and productivity levels must be available to work each shift. Foodservice managers often use a master schedule to simplify the preparation of weekly schedules. A **master schedule** is simply a spreadsheet showing the number of people needed in each position to run the foodservice operation. There are no names involved, simply the positions and the number of employees in those positions.

At the Tiki Hut, a host/cashier, a busser, a dishwasher, two cooks, and a salad person must be added to the four servers already planned to work. The master schedule would then look like the one shown in *Exhibit 4c*.

Based on this master schedule, the total payroll for one day at the Tiki Hut is $276.95. This total includes servers as well as all

Exhibit 4c

Master Schedule for the Tiki Hut

Time	8:00	9:00	10:00	11:00	12:00	1:00	2:00	Total Hours	Rate	Total Payroll
Covers			15	75	80	90	40			
Position										
Server A			✗	✗	✗	✗	✗	5	$ 2.13	$ 10.65
Server B				✗	✗	✗	✗	4	2.13	8.52
Server C				✗	✗	✗		3	2.13	6.39
Server D				✗	✗	✗		3	2.13	6.39
Host/cashier			✗	✗	✗	✗	✗	5	$ 7.50	$ 37.50
Busser				✗	✗	✗	✗	4	6.00	24.00
Dishwasher				✗	✗	✗	✗	4	6.50	26.00
Cook 1	✗	✗	✗	✗	✗	✗		6	10.00	60.00
Cook 2		✗	✗	✗	✗	✗	✗	6	8.00	48.00
Salads	✗	✗	✗	✗	✗	✗		6	8.25	49.50
Total										**$276.95**

other hourly (variable-cost) staff. To determine the total variable payroll for the week, assume a six-day work week.

$276.95 × 6 days = $1,661.70

This weekly variable labor amount is just under the original target of $1,662 (see *Step 3* on p. 44).

Step 6: Prepare the Actual Work Schedule

Now that the master schedule has been determined, the actual crew schedule with the employees' names can be prepared. (See *Exhibit 4d.*) While at first glance this would seem like an easy task, it is important to consider each employee's knowledge of his or her job, experience level, and productivity rates. Events such as holidays and local celebrations quite often dramatically affect sales volume as well. Conversely, construction in the area would adversely affect sales. In such cases, management should adjust the number of employees from the number indicated on the master schedule.

While the task of assembling a schedule seems daunting, there are a number of software programs available to assist management. Some are stand-alone scheduling programs, and some are integrated into complete restaurant accounting programs. Most will analyze the payroll and sales records, and figure the covers per server, the average wage, and the breakdown of fixed and variable labor. While the programs perform most of the calculations automatically, it is still management's responsibility to ensure that the correct numbers of staff are scheduled to meet the forecasted sales volume.

Exhibit 4d

Crew Schedule for the Tiki Hut, Week of June 20

Name	Position	Monday	Tuesday	Wednesday	Thursday	Friday	Saturday
Brenda	Server	10–3	10–3	10–3	10–3	10–3	10–3
Sung Lee	Server	11–3	11–3	11–3	11–3	11–3	11–3
James	Server	11–2	11–2	11–2	11–2	11–2	11–2
Tony	Server	11–2	11–2	11–2	11–2	11–2	11–2
Rubin	Host/Cashier	10–3	10–3	10–3	10–3	10–3	10–3
Wendy	Busser	11–3	11–3	11–3	11–3	11–3	11–3
Mike	Dishwasher	11–3	11–3	11–3	11–3	11–3	11–3
Carlo	Cook 1	8–2	8–2	8–2	8–2	8–2	8–2
Judy	Cook 2	9–3	9–3	9–3	9–3	8–2	8–2
Tonya	Salads	8–2	8–2	8–2	8–2	8–2	8–2

Think About It...

Let's say a restaurant buys a new stove for $5,000. If the cost of the stove couldn't be depreciated, it would have to be recorded as an expense in the year it was bought. As a result, the accounting records would show a significant drop in the restaurant's profits for that year, whereas following years might show profits artificially above normal. But since the stove continues to contribute to the restaurant's sales throughout its useful life, which is five years, its cost is depreciated gradually, and the expense is spread evenly over the useful life of the stove. If the restaurant couldn't depreciate the stove, its taxes would be low the first year and much higher in the following years. With depreciation, the tax advantage of the stove's expense is spread over the useful life of the stove.

Other Costs

Many of the other costs in a operating budget, such as rent or insurance, include fixed costs that will not change from period to period. Other costs, such as entertainment or marketing, are determined by deciding what is needed and costing it out. These costs will vary and are usually specific to each operation. Again, historical records and POS reports should help managers determine other costs.

In addition, there are costs related to depreciation and taxes that are figured based on specific formulas. These calculations will vary by operation and, at times, can be fairly complicated.

Depreciation is a method of calculating and recording the reduction in value of an asset over its useful lifetime. This accounting principle lets businesses make an expensive investment without showing a big loss at the time the investment is bought.

Depreciation is also an important way that businesses manage the amount of taxes they owe, since taxes are based on a business's profit or loss in any given year. Depreciation amounts are a noncash expense included on an operation's profit and loss statement.

There are guidelines that must be followed for calculating depreciation and determining useful life estimates for items such as equipment and vehicles. These guidelines are established by the Internal Revenue Service (IRS) and generally accepted accounting principles (GAAP). As a manager, you will probably not be involved in calculating depreciation for assets purchased by your operation. However, if you are responsible to determine those calculations, you should consult with an accountant to ensure you are calculating depreciation amounts according to generally accepted accounting principles.

Putting It All Together

Now that management has determined what sales and costs are expected to be, they can estimate the expected profit or loss for the budget period. The calculation of profit or loss will be explored in detail in Chapter 5. For now, it is important to know that the expected profit or loss of an operation is simply the difference between the budgeted revenue and the budgeted costs.

Exhibit 4e, on the following pages, illustrates an operating budget for a seasonal restaurant called BeBe's Courtyard Bistro. Calculations for profit and/or loss are included in the budget and can be seen at a glance.

Exhibit 4e

Bebe's Courtyard Bistro—Operating Budget

		January	February	March	April	May	June
Sales							
Food		16,500	24,750	33,000	41,250	49,500	66,000
Beverage		5,525	8,290	11,050	13,815	16,575	22,100
	Total:	**22,025**	**33,040**	**44,050**	**55,065**	**66,075**	**88,100**
Cost of sales							
Food		6,600	9,900	13,200	16,500	19,800	26,400
Beverage		1,660	2,485	3,315	4,145	4,975	6,630
	Total:	**8,260**	**12,385**	**16,515**	**20,645**	**24,775**	**33,030**
Gross profit	Total:	**13,765**	**20,655**	**27,535**	**34,420**	**41,300**	**55,070**
Gross profit = Total sales — Total cost of sales							
Controllable expenses							
Salaries and wages		7,050	9,910	13,215	16,520	18,500	24,670
Direct		1,320	1,980	2,645	3,305	3,965	5,285
Utilities		1,250	1,250	1,250	1,250	1,250	1,250
Marketing		500	500	500	500	500	500
Administrative		1,000	1,000	1,000	1,000	1,000	1,000
Repairs and maintenance		1,000	1,000	1,000	1,000	1,000	1,000
	Total:	**12,120**	**15,640**	**19,610**	**23,575**	**26,215**	**33,705**
Noncontrollable expenses							
Occupation expenses		2,500	2,500	2,500	2,500	2,500	2,500
Interest expenses		160	215	270	270	270	270
	Total:	**2,660**	**2,715**	**2,770**	**2,770**	**2,770**	**2,770**
Total expenses	Total:	**14,780**	**18,355**	**22,380**	**26,345**	**28,985**	**36,475**
Total expenses = Controllable expenses + Noncontrollable expenses							
Operating profit	Total:	**(1,015)**	**2,300**	**5,155**	**8,075**	**12,315**	**18,595**
Operating profit = Gross profit — Total expenses							
Adjustments							
Depreciation		1,800	1,800	2,250	2,250	2,250	2,250
Amortization		1,000	1,000	1,000	1,000	1,000	1,000
	Total:	**2,800**	**2,800**	**3,250**	**3,250**	**3,250**	**3,250**
Income before taxes	Total:	**$ (3,815)**	**$ (500)**	**$ 1,905**	**$ 4,825**	**$ 9,065**	**$ 15,345**
Income before taxes = Operating profit — [Depreciation + Amortization]							

July	August	September	October	November	December		Annual Total
102,300	102,300	69,300	33,000	16,500	13,200		$ 567,600
34,255	34,255	23,205	11,050	5,525	4,420		190,065
136,555	136,555	92,505	44,050	22,025	17,620		$ 757,665
40,920	40,920	27,720	13,200	6,600	5,280		$ 227,040
10,275	10,275	6,960	3,315	1,660	1,325		57,020
51,195	51,195	34,680	16,515	8,260	6,605		$ 284,060
85,360	85,360	57,825	27,535	13,765	11,015		$ 473,605
38,235	38,235	25,900	13,215	7,050	5,640		$ 218,140
8,195	8,195	5,550	2,645	1,320	1,055		45,460
1,250	1,250	1,250	1,250	1,250	1,250		15,000
500	500	500	500	500	500		6,000
1,000	1,000	1,000	1,000	1,000	1,000		12,000
1,000	1,000	1,000	1,000	1,000	1,000		12,000
50,180	50,180	35,200	19,610	12,120	10,445		$ 308,600
2,500	2,500	2,500	2,500	2,500	2,500		$ 30,000
270	270	255	245	230	220		2,945
2,770	2,770	2,755	2,745	2,730	2,720		$ 32,945
52,950	52,950	37,955	22,355	14,850	13,165		$ 341,545
32,410	32,410	19,870	5,180	(1,085)	(2,150)		$ 132,060
2,250	2,250	2,250	2,250	2,250	2,250		$ 26,100
1,000	1,000	1,000	1,000	1,000	1,000		12,000
3,250	3,250	3,250	3,250	3,250	3,250		$ 38,100
$29,160	$29,160	$16,620	$ 1,930	$(4,335)	$ (5,400)		$ 93,960

Activity

Lucky's Operating Budget

You have just been hired as general manager of Lucky's. It is September 1, and you must prepare the operating budget of this restaurant for the first quarter of the upcoming calendar year and submit it to the corporate office. Since you have only been at the unit for a month or so, you must rely solely on historical data. You gather sales reports and records for the months of January through August of the current year.

Using this data and the budget worksheet provided, prepare the operating budget for Lucky's for the months of January through March of the upcoming year. Here is the information you determined from the most recent sales and costs records:

■ Sales are 10% higher than those of the same month during the previous year.

■ Food cost percentage is steady at 32%.

■ Fixed labor costs are steady at $9,000 per month.

■ Variable labor costs are 15% of sales.

■ Occupancy costs will remain steady at $2,000 per month.

■ Other controllable costs are expected to be $10,000 per month.

■ Marketing costs have been fixed at $1,000 per month.

■ For January, February, and March of last year, Lucky's sales revenues were as follows:
  ☐ Last year January: $60,000
  ☐ Last year February: $50,000
  ☐ Last year March: $55,000

	January	February	March
Sales			
Food			
Total sales			
Cost of sales			
Food			
Total cost of sales			
Gross profit			
Controllable expenses			
Salaries and wages			
Marketing			
Other controllable expenses			
Total controllable expenses			
Noncontrollable expenses			
Occupancy costs			
Total noncontrollable expenses			
Operating profit and income before depreciation and taxes			

Summary

An operating budget is a projected financial plan for a specific period of time. It lists the anticipated sales revenue and projected expenses, gives an estimate of the profit or loss for the period (often prepared for monthly time periods), and serves many purposes in the management of a foodservice operation.

Most operating budgets are based on forecasts. A forecast is a prediction of sales levels or costs that will occur during a specific time period. The first step in creating an operating budget is forecasting anticipated sales revenue for the operation. Operational records such as sales histories, production sheets, and popularity indexes provide this information. Using the moving average technique, information for two or three recent and similar periods is averaged together. This averaging can produce a forecast that is more likely to be accurate, since it is not based solely on one period that might have been unique. There are several software products available to calculate sales forecasts.

Once there is a reliable forecast of sales revenue, management can move forward and forecast costs for the budget period. Past history is key to accurate cost forecasting as well. Managers should use any available records and tools to analyze historical cost data.

In general, the three categories of costs for a foodservice operation are food costs, labor costs, and other costs (also known as "overhead"). The key to forecasting food costs is to know the target food cost percentage. As long as you have a sales forecast and a target food cost percentage, the calculation of the forecasted food costs is straightforward.

Anticipated labor costs can be complicated to calculate. Fortunately, there is a step-by-step process that managers can follow. This process includes determining labor dollars available and distributing them among staff positions to create a schedule. There are also a number of software programs available to assist managers.

Many of the other costs in a budget, such as rent or insurance, include fixed costs that will not change from period to period. Other costs, such as marketing, are determined by deciding what is needed and costing it out. These costs will vary and are usually specific to each operation. Again, historical records and POS reports help you determine these.

Once management has determined what income and costs are expected to be, they can compile the actual operating budget and estimate the expected profit or loss for the budget period.

Review Your Learning

1 Which of the following is *not* a purpose of operating budgets?

A. Plan for staffing needs

B. Anticipate labor turnover

C. Measure actual performance

D. Outline performance goals for management

2 Which is another term for forecast?

A. Plan

B. Data

C. Intuition

D. Prediction

3 Production sheets are a tool for measuring

A. payroll costs.

B. actual revenue.

C. standard portion cost.

D. menu item popularity.

4 Which cost is *most* difficult to budget?

A. Food

B. Labor

C. Utilities

D. Inventory

5 In order to determine the amount of money that can be spent on hourly employees for the period, what must be subtracted from total labor dollars?

A. Salary wages

B. Fixed-cost payroll

C. Benefits and deductions

D. All of the above

6 Which of the following is *true* regarding master schedules?

A. Some operations require more than one master schedule.

B. The master schedule should not be adjusted for any reason.

C. The master schedule is used to prepare only front-of-the-house staff schedules.

D. Only the most competent and experienced staff members are included on the master schedule.

The Profit and Loss Report

Inside This Chapter

- What Is a Profit and Loss Report?

- Preparing Profit and Loss Reports

- Analyzing Profit and Loss Reports

After completing this chapter, you should be able to:

- Describe a profit and loss report, and explain its use.

- Prepare a profit and loss report based on sales and cost information.

- Analyze information found on a profit and loss report.

Test Your Knowledge

1 **True or False:** Another name for the profit and loss report is the *income statement.* *(See p. 56.)*

2 **True or False:** An operation has made a profit when its expenses are equal to its income. *(See p. 58.)*

3 **True or False:** It is important to manually check the calculations of any reports run from POS systems. *(See p. 57.)*

4 **True or False:** The total amount of taxes paid by an operation is referred to as "the bottom line." *(See p. 58.)*

5 **True or False:** A variance in costs between two similar periods might indicate a problem. *(See p. 59.)*

Key Terms

Income statement

Loss

Profit

Profit and loss report

Sales

Variance

Introduction

How can a foodservice manager quickly assess the status of an operation's finances? The best way to see at a glance how the operation is performing is by reading its profit and loss report. The profit and loss report provides a brief snapshot of the operation's financial activity. Profit and loss reports also provide financial data that is used in turn to analyze trends and identify areas for improvement.

What Is a Profit and Loss Report?

In simple terms, a **profit and loss report** is a compilation of sales and cost information for a specific period of time. This report shows whether an operation has made or lost money during the time period covered by the report.

The profit and loss report, which is also called the **income statement,** is a valuable management tool. It helps managers gauge an operation's profitability as well as compare actual results to expected goals. Carefully monitoring this information periodically— such as monthly or quarterly—helps management determine areas where adjustments must be made to bring business operations in line with established financial goals.

An example of a profit and loss report appears in *Exhibit 5b* on p. 57. Note how the report is organized. It lists sales income first, then lists all expenses. The end of the report reflects the amount of profit or loss for the period covered.

Preparing Profit and Loss Reports

Step 1: Determine Time Period for Report

The first step in preparing a profit and loss report is to determine what time period the report should cover. Once that is decided, the financial records should be gathered. Accurate data is important. Most point-of-sale (POS) systems can generate reports directly from computerized sales and accounting records, avoiding the need for manually looking up and calculating the data.

Step 2: Calculate Total Sales

The next step in preparing a profit and loss report is to figure out total sales for the period selected. **Sales** includes all of the income the restaurant has made in the given time period. This can be done by totaling receipts for each category, such as food or beverage. Some restaurants also sell merchandise—such as souvenir T-shirts and other specialty products—which might have their own sales category. Then, these categories are added together to calculate the total sales for a certain period. Sales information can be broken down even further. Many operations will also separate their sales by types—like catering or banquets.

Step 3: Calculate Total Costs

Next, total costs—or expenses—need to be calculated for the same period. These costs might include invoices paid, payroll reports, or accruals. Expenses can be determined from either paper records or through the POS system reports. For example, labor cost can be determined by reviewing payroll reports.

As discussed in Chapter 3, there are various categories of costs, including controllable or noncontrollable costs, and also variable, semivariable, or fixed costs. Because fixed expenses do not change regularly, managers only need to figure out fixed expenses for a set time period to determine the cost of those expenses over a greater period of time. For instance, if a manager wants to know the yearly expense of a fixed rent, all that needs to be done is multiplying the monthly rent expense by twelve to determine the total yearly cost.

Exhibit 5a

Types of Taxes

Taxes Due from the Operation

■ **Income taxes.** These can be federal, state, or local.

■ **Property taxes.** Real property taxes can be a major expense and may be imposed by state or local jurisdictions. They are based on the assessed value of the property.

■ **Personal property taxes.** This could include such categories as kitchen equipment and improvements; small wares such as china, glassware, and dining room equipment; and construction in progress.

Taxes Collected by the Operation on Behalf of the Government

■ **Sales taxes.** Most states have some sort of sales and use tax. Although it is paid by customers, it is collected by sellers.

■ **Payroll taxes.** These can be considered in two categories. One is tax money withheld from employees' paychecks and then paid to the government by the employer. These taxes are also paid by the employee. The other payroll taxes include federal unemployment insurance, workers' compensation, and unemployment compensation.

Taxes

Another item usually included in costs is taxes. Taxes are a cost of doing business that most operations must pay. Taxes must be paid and records kept for those taxes. A business could have many types of taxes, including those from the local, state, and federal government. These include the types listed in *Exhibit 5a.*

Step 4: Subtract Total Costs from Total Sales

The profit or loss of a restaurant operation is simply the difference between the total sales (or income) and the total costs (or expenses). This figure, found at the end of the profit and loss report, is also known as "the bottom line." If sales are higher than costs, then the operation is making a **profit.** Conversely, if the total costs are higher than the total sales, then the restaurant is running at a **loss** for the specified time period.

If you look at the example in *Exhibit 5b*, you can see that Rancher's Steak House made a profit of $6,200 for the month of April 2008.

Activity

Income or Expense?

Classify each of the items listed below as either *income* (I) or *expense* (E).

_____ **1** Revenue from T-Shirt sales

_____ **2** Wages

_____ **3** Marketing

_____ **4** Food Sales

_____ **5** Utilities

Exhibit 5b

Rancher's Steak House Profit and Loss Report

For the Period: 4/1/08 to 4/30/08

Sales

Food	$ 80,000
Beverage	20,000
Total sales	$100,000

Cost of Sales

Food	$ 32,000
Beverage	5,000
Total cost of sales	$ 37,000

Gross Profit

Food	$ 48,000
Beverage	15,000
Total gross profit	$ 63,000

Controllable Expenses

Salaries and wages	$ 26,000
Employee benefits	4,000
Legal/accounting	500
Music and entertainment	5,000
Marketing	250
Utility services	2,000
General and administrative	3,800
Repairs and maintenance	2,000
Other income	250
Total controllable expenses	$ 43,800

Fixed Expenses

Rent	$ 5,700
Depreciation	1,000
Utility services	0
Licenses/permits	100
Insurance	3,000
Loan payments	2,500
Total fixed expenses	$ 12,300

Profit/(Loss)*	$ 6,900
Income Taxes	$ 700
Net Earning (Loss)	$ 6,200

*before income taxes

Analyzing Profit and Loss Reports

Managers collect profit and loss data on their operations for a purpose. Most larger organizations have an internal auditing staff that sets the requirements for such financial reporting. Investors, owners, and managers look carefully at these reports to determine the profitability of an operation. The reports might also be used to judge the efficiency of an operation, to determine where costs have gotten out of line, and to make basic management decisions.

There are several approaches to analyzing a profit and loss report. When comparing a recent profit and loss report to the budget, company standards, industry standards, or historical trends, you need to be looking for any variances—changes that have occurred. This is a good way to check how the operation is running and can prevent future problems by catching them early. As soon as variances are observed, you should analyze what happened and develop a plan of how to correct the problem.

Comparing Actual Values to Budgeted Values

Profit and loss reports are useful when comparing what is actually occurring to what was budgeted or planned for. Any variance between actual amounts and the budget could indicate that something unexpected has occurred. For instance, actual sales amounts might not be as high as were expected due to bad weather conditions or emergency road repairs in front of the operation. It is easy to see where such unforeseen conditions have affected sales.

In addition, variances might indicate that the assumptions made during creation of the budget were inaccurate. If this is the case, you will want to take a closer look at these assumptions when preparing future budgets.

Comparing Actual Values to Standards

Most restaurants will have standards to compare to as well. These standards are usually the basis of the operation's original budget. General industry standards reflect accepted ranges for certain costs within the foodservice industry. These standards are not an exact measurement. It is important to make sure the values being compared actually fit the nature of an operation. For example, a fine-dining restaurant will have a higher percentage of labor costs than a quick-service restaurant. If the fine-dining manager's goal is to have better service than any other restaurant in the area, then the operation should expect to have labor costs that are higher than the industry standard.

If an operation is part of a chain, there will likely be company standards to compare against. Company standards are used as a guide for how the operation can and should be run. This includes percentages of costs coming from food and beverage. It also could be broken down more specifically into certain food items. Other controllable and fixed expenses can be addressed by company standards as well.

Comparing Actual Values to Historical Trends

Another way to analyze the information on a profit and loss report is to compare it with historical data from the operation. This can be done for an individual unit or across multiple properties. Using historical trends is a great way to look for seasonal changes. It can also be used to remind managers of upcoming local events that had an effect on a previous year's sales.

Activity

Dare to Compare

Identify whether each of the following is an example of an industry standard (I), company standard (C), or historical trend (H).

_____ **1** All John's Deli franchises should keep food cost below 25 percent.

_____ **2** Most quick-service operations have a food cost of lower than 22 percent.

_____ **3** A cost variance of more than 10 percent between two periods in a row must be reported.

_____ **4** At the Florida Inn in Miami, sales during the month of August are typically half of what they are in December.

_____ **5** Our target for next period is to reduce food cost by 1 percent.

Activity

Late Night at the Diner

It is 8:00 p.m. on a snowy Sunday night at Derek's Family Diner. The restaurant has very few customers—the basketball team from the local high school is playing in the finals of the state tournament, which is being broadcast on cable. Carl, the night manager, decides to cut two of the five servers from the floor early. They finish their sidework and clock out at 8:30 p.m. At about 9:20 p.m., a steady stream of people come into the diner—several large parties at the same time. Carl learns that the arts center down the street presented its opening night performance of "A Star-Filled Holiday," and most of the customers have come to enjoy coffee and pie before the diner closes at 10:00 p.m.

Given this information, answer the following:

1 What effect will these factors have on the profit and loss report for Derek's Family Diner for this week?

_____

_____

_____

_____

2 How might this period's report vary from those of previous periods?

_____

_____

_____

_____

Summary

In simple terms, a profit and loss report is a compilation of sales and cost information for a specific period of time. This report shows whether an operation has made or lost money during the time period covered by the report.

The profit and loss report, which is also called the income statement, is a valuable management tool. It helps managers gauge an operation's profitability as well as compare actual results to expected goals. Careful, periodic monitoring of this information—such as monthly or quarterly—helps management determine areas where adjustments must be made to bring business operations in line with established goals.

The profit and loss report lists sales income first. It then lists all expenses. The end of the report reflects the amount of profit or loss for the period covered. If sales are higher than costs, then the operation is making a profit. Conversely, if the total costs are higher than the total sales, the restaurant is running at a loss for the specified time period.

The first step in preparing a profit and loss report is to determine what time period the report should cover. Once that is decided, the financial records should be gathered. The next step is to figure out total sales for the period selected. Then, total costs, or expenses, need to be calculated for the same period. The profit or loss of a restaurant operation is simply the difference between the total sales (or income) and the total costs (or expenses).

Management looks carefully at profit and loss reports to determine the profitability of an operation, to judge the operation's efficiency, to determine where costs have gotten out of line, and to make basic management decisions.

There are several approaches to analyzing a profit and loss report. When a manager is comparing a recent profit and loss report to the budget, company standards, industry standards, or historical trends, he or she needs to be looking for any variances or changes that have occurred. This is a good way to check how the operation is running and can prevent future problems by catching them early. As soon as variances are observed, the manager should develop a plan of how to correct the problem.

Review Your Learning

1 The profit and loss report is also called the

A. balance sheet.

B. income statement.

C. bottom line statement.

D. statement of net worth.

2 Which is the correct formula for calculating profit or loss?

A. Monthly sales × 12

B. Total costs − Total sales

C. Total sales − Total costs

D. Annual sales − Monthly costs

3 What is the *final step* in preparing a profit and loss report?

A. Calculate total sales.

B. Calculate total costs.

C. Subtract total costs from total sales.

D. Determine what time period the report should cover.

4 What information is included at the top of a profit and loss report?

A. Sales

B. Costs

C. Taxes

D. Expenses

5 Which of the following *are not* commonly compared to profit and loss reports?

A. Historical trends

B. Company standards

C. Operational budgets

D. Customer service surveys

6 An operation's budget lists food expenses as $14,000. The profit and loss report for the period indicates food expenses were $18,000. What has occurred?

A. Variance

B. Tolerance

C. Standard deviation

D. Corrective action

Notes

Introduction to Cost Control

Inside This Chapter

- The Cost Control Process
- A Closer Look at Costs

After completing this chapter, you should be able to:

- Explain the basic foodservice cost control process.
- Calculate food cost and food cost percentage.
- Analyze food product waste.
- Evaluate inventory performance and productivity.
- Calculate labor cost and labor cost percentage.
- Calculate labor productivity ratios, including sales per labor hour, average wage per hour, covers per hour, and sales per cover.

Test Your Knowledge

1. **True or False:** An operating budget is a tool used in cost control. *(See pp. 66–69.)*

2. **True or False:** After a line item review of costs has been performed, variances can be identified and analyzed. *(See pp. 67–68.)*

3. **True or False:** Food cost percentage is a measurement of the relationship between actual sales and the cost of food sold during the same period. *(See p. 71.)*

4. **True or False:** Labor costs include employee wages only, not the cost of employee benefits. *(See p. 73.)*

5. **True or False:** Performance and productivity ratios are used to evaluate and analyze labor costs. *(See p. 73.)*

Key Terms

Corrective action

Cover

Food product waste

Labor cost

Labor cost percentage

Line item review

Payroll cost

Introduction

Controlling and reducing costs are both desirable trends for ensuring the ongoing financial health of a foodservice operation. Taking action to reduce operating costs depends on understanding which costs might be out of line and what can be done to correct them. At the same time, any adjustments made to control costs must ensure continuation of the operation's expected levels of safety, sanitation, and customer service.

With experience, managers learn to quickly spot cost control concerns in their operations. Other cost control analyses take a more detailed approach to evaluate and correct. Volumes of guidelines and other information are available to help foodservice managers in their cost control efforts.

The Cost Control Process

As reviewed in Chapter 4, the operating budget is the financial plan for a foodservice operation. It clearly outlines the financial targets related to both sales and costs. If a budget is planned carefully, the future should not hold too many surprises. But to make sure of this, the process of controlling costs begins right where the budgeting process leaves off.

Step 1: Collect Accurate Sales and Cost Data

Historical sales information is just as important to cost control as it is to other management functions. The relationship between sales and the costs that were incurred to achieve those actual sales is often proportional, and many foodservice costs change depending on sales volume. In order to know whether costs are within an appropriate range, it is imperative to start with accurate sales information.

Sales should be tracked for different periods, including yearly, monthly, weekly, daily, meal period, and even hourly.

- Yearly and monthly data are used for budgeting and income statement purposes.

- Weekly and daily sales information is used for purchasing and scheduling.

- Daily and meal period data are also used for scheduling as well as for production planning.

Sales information can come from several sources. Yearly and monthly sales information comes from the income statement. Hourly, daily, and weekly figures are usually generated by point-of-sale (POS) system reports. In operations that do not have POS systems, this information comes from tabulating guest checks or periodic cash register readings.

In addition to having accurate sales information, it is also necessary to have accurate cost information. Most cost information can be taken from operational records. Many POS systems function to track inventory, food waste, and employee work hours. Management can usually run reports of inventory and food costs, payroll costs, and actual labor hours.

Step 2: Monitor and Analyze Sales and Costs

Once actual sales and costs are calculated, these figures are monitored and compared to budgeted amounts, operational standards, and historical information in order to identify any variances. This monitoring should be done on a regular and ongoing basis. This is a good way to check how the operation is running and can prevent future problems by catching them early.

Every item on the budget should be checked, if possible, against actual figures, and the difference should be noted. This is called a **line item review.** When the budget is compared to the actual sales figures, the numbers for each item should be identical or at least very close to each other. Any difference between the budget and the actual amounts may be expressed as a dollar amount and/or a percentage.

A format for comparing budgeted and actual amounts using a line item review is illustrated in *Exhibit 6a*.

Exhibit 6a

Sample Line Item Review

Budget Item	$ Budgeted	$ Actual	$ Difference	% Difference
Food sales	$100,000	$90,000	$10,000	–10%

As discussed in Chapter 4, all restaurant chains and most independent restaurant operators have standards or goals they want to achieve. In the case of controlling costs, the standard represents the level at which a cost *should be*. Standard costs are carefully calculated to ensure that the operation achieves profitability while at the same time maintaining expected customer service levels.

For example, an operation should always be concerned about maintaining proper customer service levels. This requires the operation to have the appropriate level of labor on site at all times. With this consideration, management compares the actual labor cost percentage to the standard labor cost percentage for the operation. The standard labor cost percentage, if determined correctly, takes into account the level of service at which management expects its operations to perform. Sufficient hours scheduled in the kitchen will result in an excellent product being sent out in a prompt manner. Likewise, the correct number of servers in the dining room to take orders and serve in an efficient manner will carry out the company's mission of good food and good service.

Remember that management determines a standard based on many factors, not the least of which is profit. When considering a labor standard, management takes into account producing a quality product and providing quality service. To go below the standard could sacrifice product or service excellence. For this reason, it is just as important to come up to the standard as it is to come down to the standard.

In addition to comparing actual costs to standard costs, management also compares actual costs to historical costs. Historical costs are those costs that have been incurred in the past. By comparing these two figures, management can see if the operation is improving or regressing.

When comparing actual costs to historical costs, it is important to remember that similar periods must be compared. Thus, January's labor cost is compared to January's labor cost of the previous year, or Monday's sales this week are compared to Monday's sales of last week ago. Special events or unusual circumstances should also be taken into account when comparing historical costs. For example, comparing this Sunday's sales to last Sunday's sales, which happened to be Mother's Day, would not be a good comparison. A heavy noontime rainstorm could increase the sales in an employee cafeteria located in an office building, and decrease the sales in a restaurant across the street from the building.

Exhibit 6b

Sample Corrective Actions for Cost Control

To Reduce	Implement These Corrective Actions
Food cost	■ Reduce portion size
	■ Replace food with more cost-effective ingredient
	■ Feature items with higher profit margins
	■ Raise menu prices
Food waste	■ Monitor portion control
	■ Monitor food storage and rotation
	■ Monitor food ordering
	■ Improve order communication to reduce production errors
Inventory cost	■ Order appropriate quantities—avoid having too much or too little in storage
Labor cost	■ Reduce number of employees on schedule
	■ Ask employees to end their shifts early
	■ Schedule cross-trained staff (for example, server/cashier/hostess)

Step 3: Take Corrective Action as Appropriate

Over time, even small changes in costs can add up to significant losses. When costs are determined to be out of line, the cause should be investigated. If the budget and actual values do not match, they must be analyzed to see what might have gone wrong. If there is a variance, management should take action to correct the variance. For example, if food cost is off, purchasing, preparation, and receiving procedures should be investigated. If labor cost show a variance, scheduling and work production standards should be analyzed.

As soon as the cause for a variance is identified, the manager should take steps to correct the problem. These steps are called **corrective actions.** As discussed in Chapter 3, foodservice managers have more control over some costs than they do over others. Corrective actions, by nature, can only be used to affect controllable costs.

For example, if sales are lower than expected, the hours included on the employee work schedule might need to be reduced to lower labor costs. *Exhibit 6b* lists some examples of corrective actions that can be taken to control various costs.

In addition to taking corrective actions, it may also be necessary to reforecast and make changes to the operations budget. As circumstances change, some forecasts used to prepare the original budget may no longer be accurate. Reviewing forecasts, at least on a monthly basis, will help managers make realistic adjustments to the budget for upcoming periods.

A Closer Look at Costs

The two largest expenses in any foodservice operation are food cost and labor cost. Both can have immediate impact on an operation's ability to make a profit. For this reason, management must focus efforts specifically to keep these two costs under control.

Food Cost

Food cost information is usually determined by reviewing inventory and purchasing records for a period. Most foodservice operations calculate food cost on a monthly basis, though some quick-service operations will do so as often as weekly.

Many people, including some foodservice managers, have the misconception that when food is purchased it becomes food cost. This is not true. Purchases certainly are an integral part of food cost; however, food cost is, in reality, the dollar value of the food that was actually used during a certain period. In the foodservice industry, the terms *food cost* and *cost of food sold* are interchangeable.

Fortunately, there is a formula for figuring food cost that takes into account the multiple purchases of multiple items in a typical restaurant. To determine the value of the food that has been used, you must have opening and closing inventory data. Then, food cost is calculated as follows:

Think About It...

When would using a lower-quality ingredient in a menu item not be a good idea, even if it does result in lower food cost?

| Value of food inventory on hand at beginning of period | + | Purchases of food during period | = | Total value of available food | − | Value of food inventory on hand at end of period | = | Food cost for period |

Exhibit 6c

Calculation of Food Cost for One Month

	$1,000	Value of food inventory on hand at beginning of month
+	$5,000	Purchases of food during month
=	$6,000	Total value of available food
−	$2,000	Value of food inventory on hand at end of month
=	$4,000	Food cost

Exhibit 6c shows how the food cost would be calculated if, for example, opening food inventory was valued at $1,000, food purchases were $5,000, and closing food inventory was valued at $2,000. When one period ends, a new period begins. In other words, the closing inventory for one period is actually the opening inventory for the next.

Food Cost Percentage

Now that the actual cost of food has been determined, the next step is to calculate the actual food cost percentage. As explained in Chapter 4, food cost percentage is a measurement of the relationship between sales and the cost spent on food in order to generate those sales. Once you have actual food cost information, food cost percentage is calculated using the following formula:

Food cost ÷ Sales = Food cost percentage

For example, if a restaurant's sales are $24,000 for a given week, and the food cost is $7,000 for the same week, then the food cost percentage for that week is 29.2%.

$7,000 ÷ $24,000 = .292 or 29.2%

Another way to state this is to say that out of every dollar of sales, food cost accounted for about $0.29.

Activity

Calculating Food Cost Percentage

Calculate the food cost percentage for each of the examples listed.

1 Breakfast sales for last week equal $17,000. To prepare the breakfast items for the week, the food cost was $2,900. What is the food cost percentage for breakfast last week?

_____

2 Shrimp cocktail has a food cost of $3.65 per order and is listed on the menu at a sales price of $9.50. What is the food cost percentage for shrimp cocktail?

_____

3 A. A sandwich shop menu lists seventeen sandwiches that vary in price from $2.79 to $6.49. If total sales for the period are $8,500, and the average sales price per sandwich is $5.00, about how many sandwiches sold during this period?

_____

B. Using the same information, assume that the average food cost per sandwich is $1.19. What is the average food cost percentage per sandwich?

_____

C. What is the total food cost for the period?

_____

The example provided indicates an average food cost percentage for a given period. This calculation can be broken down into further levels of detail, such as menu item, menu category, or even meal period. For instance, the average breakfast food cost percentage might be lower than the average dinner food cost percentage. As with any measurement, food cost percentage is most often compared to the company standard, historical costs, or even industry standards.

Food Product Waste

Another important expense directly related to food cost is **food product waste.** Food product waste is a measurement of how much food product is taken from inventory but not actually sold. This waste figure includes costs for mistakes made during preparation, food that must be discarded, or food items that have been stolen or misused by staff. Food product waste is also called "shrinkage."

Measuring the cost of food product waste is important, as it helps managers identify where steps must be taken to reduce waste. Food product waste can be determined by comparing sales reports to the actual amount of food product inventory used. Items that have been used, but are not included in the sales report, are usually considered waste.

For example, if sales reports indicate that twenty strip steaks were sold, yet the inventory records show twenty-five steaks were actually taken from inventory, then five steaks are missing and considered wasted. If each steak costs the operation $2.07, then the food product waste for strip steaks is $10.35 for the period.

Some waste cannot be avoided, and most operations expect to have at least some waste over time. Obviously, the most perishable and expensive food products are at higher risk for resulting in higher waste costs, as just a few mistakes can be very costly. Whether or not waste amounts are acceptable can be determined by comparing actual waste amounts to ideal, or standard, waste figures. This comparison between actual costs and ideal costs, or standards, can be performed for both total waste and product cost. Such standards will vary by type of operation and menu items.

There are several techniques that can be used to help prevent or reduce food product waste. *Exhibit 6d* lists a few of these techniques. There are countless other waste-reduction practices in place in the foodservice industry.

Think About It...

What are some other ways a manager can reduce product waste costs?

Exhibit 6d

Tips for Reducing Food Product Waste

- Set ideal values of prep items to avoid overproduction.

- Track ordering and cooking mistakes. This will help pinpoint food waste problems or patterns.

- Reuse product scraps and leftovers where appropriate. For example, turn day-old bread into homemade salad croutons.

- Store food items at the correct temperatures to prevent spoilage.

- Keep inventory of food items secure—lock storerooms and freezers.

Labor Cost

Often, the terms *labor cost* and *payroll cost* are used interchangeably in the restaurant industry. They are, in reality, two different things. **Payroll cost** is the amount of money that is spent for employee wages, both fixed and variable. **Labor cost** is all-inclusive and includes, in addition to payroll cost, such costs as the employer's contribution to FICA and Medicare, workers' compensation insurance, and employee benefits. All of these are integral parts of labor cost and should be calculated into the labor cost total.

When labor cost is determined to be out of line, corrective actions can include reforecasting the labor budget and adjusting the work schedules. Managers can use a variety of techniques to analyze labor costs.

Total Hours Worked

If sales are fairly consistent from week-to-week or month-to-month, then the total hours worked for each period will provide accurate information to analyze. If, however, sales fluctuate from day-to-day, week-to-week, or month-to-month, this tool loses its validity.

For example, the manager of a hospital foodservice department that has a consistent patient count can compare the total hours worked from one week to the next to see if the labor cost is on budget. Conversely, the manager of a restaurant across the street from a convention center cannot use this method, as the sales vary greatly each period depending on the number of events booked at the center.

However, in a well-operated restaurant, it goes much further than just adding all these costs together to find the labor total. There are several ways to evaluate labor cost. Performance and productivity ratios provide added detail in order to perform accurate and meaningful analysis. Some of the more common calculations for measuring and analyzing labor cost include those listed in *Exhibit 6e*. Each of these deserves a closer look.

Labor Cost Percentage

When analyzing labor cost, it is important to convert it into a percentage. To simply look at the dollars spent is to see only part of the picture. By looking at labor cost as a percentage, the relationship between the labor cost and sales is taken into account. Labor cost is converted into a **labor cost percentage** by dividing the actual labor cost by sales as shown in the following formula:

Labor cost ÷ Sales = Labor cost percentage

Exhibit 6e

Performance and Productivity Ratios Used to Analyze Labor Cost

- Labor cost percentage
- Sales per labor hour
- Average wage per hour
- Covers per hour
- Sales per cover

For example, if a restaurant's sales are $12,000 for a given week and the labor cost is $4,000 for the same week, then the labor cost percentage for that week is 33.3%.

$4,000 ÷ $12,000 = .333 or 33.3%

While most operations look at labor cost percentage monthly, many will analyze labor cost percent weekly and some will even do it daily. Analyzing labor cost percentages daily can ultimately produce positive results. If the daily percentage is in line, then the weekly will be in line, as will the monthly. By looking at daily figures, action can be taken immediately to remedy the cost if it is not to the norm.

When analyzing labor cost percentage, the results are most often compared to the company standard. They can, however, be compared to historical costs, and can also be compared to industry standards. Caution should be exercised when comparing to industry standards, however, as restaurant operations differ greatly. Urban versus rural, union versus nonunion, self-service versus full-service, complexity of the menu, and different sections of the country all have an effect on labor cost. In other words, it costs more to provide fine-dining table service than it does to provide walk-up counter service, so general industry standards for labor cost percentage can be misleading.

Sales per Labor Hour

Sales per labor hour gives an indication of how productive the staff is. Sales per labor hour is normally figured for hourly, or variable-cost employees only, since salaried employees normally do not work a fixed number of hours, but rather put in the hours necessary to get the job done. Hourly employees, on the other hand, are paid for the actual number of hours they work.

Sales per labor hour can be figured for any sales period: hour, meal, day, week, month, or year. To calculate sales per labor hour, take the sales for a period and divide by the number of hours worked for that same period.

Sales ÷ Number of hours worked = Sales per labor hour

For example, if sales for April are $60,000, and the number of hours worked by hourly employees is 300, then the sales per labor hour is $200.

$60,000 ÷ 300 hours = $200

If sales per labor hour drops, some questions should be asked. Are the tables being turned over quickly enough? Is the host seating patrons in an orderly fashion? Are the bussers performing to standard? Is the wait staff taking orders quickly? Is the wait staff selling or merely taking orders? Are the cooks turning the orders out of the kitchen in a timely manner? At the same time, it is entirely possible that a drop in sales per labor hour could simply be due to a drop in sales, and not staff performance.

Average Wage per Hour

Like sales per labor hour, the average wage per hour is normally figured for variable-cost (hourly) employees only. To figure the average wage per hour, take the total variable labor cost and divide it by the total number of hours worked by the hourly employees.

$$\text{Total variable labor cost} \div \text{Number of hours worked by variable cost employees} = \text{Average wage per hour}$$

For example, if the total variable payroll costs for October are $30,000, and the number of hours worked by hourly employees is 4,000 hours, then the average wage per hour is $7.50.

$$\$30,000 \div 4,000 \text{ hours} = \$7.50$$

Quite often, the average wage per hour is broken down by department, such as front of the house and back of the house. Front of the house can then be separated into wait staff, host/hostess, and bartenders, while back of the house could be broken down into cooks and dishwashers. Looking carefully at each department and position helps management determine more clearly where scheduling problems are occurring. Also, there is a rather large wage gap among job classifications. For example, line cooks might average $10 per hour, while the wait staff might average $4 per hour because they receive tips. Calculating a single figure for all of these wage groups together could give a distorted average.

Average wage per hour can be used to compare wages in one restaurant against the community standard. For example, one restaurant pays an average of $7.00 for line cooks, and the other restaurants in the area are paying an average of $9.50. This could explain why one particular restaurant has a high turnover of line cooks. As noted in Chapter 4, average wage per hour is also useful in the budgeting process and for preparing work schedules.

Covers per Hour and Sales per Cover

When analyzed together, covers per hour and sales per cover will indicate who the best servers are in terms of productivity (table turnover) and sales ability (high average check). These numbers can be used to develop a standard by which all servers are measured.

Exhibit 6f

Covers per hour will vary based on type of operation productivity, service style, and individual server.

Covers per hour is a measure of a wait person's productivity. In figuring covers per hour, one **cover** is equal to one customer meal served. (See *Exhibit 6f.*)Thus, covers per hour could also be expressed as *customer meals served per hour.* To calculate covers per hour, take the number of covers served by a waitperson (for a shift, day, week, or month) and divide by the number of hours that person worked.

Number of covers ÷ Hours = Covers per hour

For example, Sue Ellen worked 30 hours last week and served 575 covers or customer meals.

575 covers ÷ 30 hours = 19.2 covers per hour

Contrast this to Carlos who worked 35 hours and served 600 covers.

600 covers ÷ 35 hours = 17.1 covers per hour

Based on this information, Sue Ellen was able to serve more customers per hour (on average) than Carlos.

Sales per cover measures the sales ability of a waitperson. The higher the figure, the more that person is selling, on average, to each customer. Sales per cover can be figured by the hour, shift, day, week, month, or year. To figure sales per cover, take the total sales for the server and divide by number of covers sold by the server.

Total sales ÷ Number of covers = Sales per
per server   sold by server   cover

To illustrate sales per cover, assume that LaToya had sales of $900 last Saturday evening and served 55 covers.

$900 ÷ 55 covers = $16.36 per cover

Contrast this to Hunter, who had $1,050 in sales for the same meal period and served 70 covers. This means LaToya sold more to each of her customers than Hunter did to his.

$1,050 ÷ 70 covers = $15.00 per cover

Even though Hunter had a higher sales total and served more customers, his sales per cover was lower than LaToya's.

Conclusions on server productivity and performance should not be drawn from one week's numbers. Analysis should be done over a period of time, as there are too many external factors that could distort figures for one shift. For example, a server who normally has a high number of covers per server rate could have a shift where several guests are content to sit and talk, consequently lowering that server's table turnover. Keep in mind that the covers per hour and sales per cover also need to be compared for the same time period. To compare one server's lunch sales with another server's dinner sales would give a distorted figure, as average lunch checks are generally lower than average dinner checks.

Another use for analyzing covers per server is to schedule the wait staff. As you read in Chapter 4, by anticipating the total number of covers to be sold for a particular meal period, management can determine the number of servers to schedule.

Activity

Sunshine Hospital Cafeteria

Gary is the manager of the cafeteria at Sunshine Hospital. He is reviewing the sales and cost records for the months of June and July. His manager has provided him with a few cost control standards for the cafeteria so that Gary can accurately analyze this information.

	June		July	
Sales		$ 19,700		$ 16,900
Opening inventory	June 1	$ 13,000	July 1	$ 14,105
Closing inventory	June 30	$ 14,105	July 31	$ 17,105
Food purchases		$ 8,000		$ 6,500
Labor expenses		$ 5,000		$ 5,000

Sunshine Hospital Cost Control Standards

■ Labor cost should be between 24% and 26%.

■ Food cost percentage should be lower than 32%.

Given this information, answer the following questions.

1 What is the cafeteria's labor cost percentage for June? For July?

_____   _____

2 What is the cafeteria's food cost for June? For July?

_____   _____

3 What is the cafeteria's food cost percentage for June? For July?

_____   _____

4 Which costs were outside of acceptable standards during either June or July?

_____   _____

5 What recommendations should Gary propose to control costs in the upcoming months?

_____   _____

Summary

The process of controlling costs begins right where the budgeting process left off. Taking action to reduce operating costs depends on understanding which costs might be out of line and what can be done to correct them. With experience, managers learn to quickly spot cost control concerns in their operations.

The relationship between sales and the costs that were incurred to achieve those actual sales is often proportional, and many foodservice costs change depending on sales volume. In order to know whether costs are in an appropriate range, it is imperative to start with accurate sales information. In addition to having accurate sales information, it is also necessary to have accurate cost information.

Once actual sales and costs are calculated, these figures are monitored and compared to budgeted amounts, operational standards, and historical information in order to identify any variances. This monitoring should be done on a regular and ongoing basis. This is a good way to check how the operation is running and can prevent future problems by catching them early. As soon as variances are observed, the manager should develop a plan of how to correct the problem. Over time, even small changes in costs can add up to significant losses or profits.

The two largest expenses in any foodservice operation are food cost and labor cost, and both can have an immediate impact on an operation's ability to make a profit. For this reason, managers must focus their efforts to keep these two costs under control.

There are several ways to evaluate food and labor costs. Food cost is often measured by comparing standards to actual food cost percentages. Waste and inventory productivity affect food cost as well. Performance and productivity ratios provide added details in order to perform accurate and meaningful labor cost analysis. These ratios include labor cost percentage, sales per labor hour, average wage per hour, covers per hour, and sales per cover.

Review Your Learning

1 Which of the following is the *first* step in the foodservice cost control process?

A. Analyze costs

B. Take corrective action

C. Prepare a line item review

D. Collect sales and cost data

2 Analyzing costs includes which of the following comparisons?

A. Comparison between actual costs and standard costs

B. Comparison between actual costs and historical costs

C. Comparison between actual costs and budgeted costs

D. All of the above

3 Food cost is *most often* calculated

A. per meal period.
C. weekly.

B. daily.
D. monthly.

4 If the beginning food inventory is valued at $15,500, food purchases are $11,000, and closing food inventory is valued at $9,800, what is the food cost for the period?

A. $16,200
C. $17,000

B. $16,700
D. $17,500

5 If food cost for a period is $3,400, and sales are $13,500, what is the food cost percentage?

A. 19.9%
C. 26.0%

B. 25.2%
D. 39.7%

6 Food items that are taken from inventory but not actually sold are considered

A. mistakes.
C. employee meals.

B. perishables.
D. food product waste.

7 Which of the following contributes to high food product waste?

A. Theft
C. Spoilage

B. Mistakes
D. All of the above

8 Which of the following is *true* about total hours worked?

A. The total hours worked are always equal to labor cost.

B. If all servers have the same skill level, total hours worked will not vary by period.

C. Payroll and labor costs are included in calculations for total hours worked.

D. If sales are consistent, the total hours worked can be an accurate measure of labor cost.

9 What is the formula for labor cost percentage?

A. Sales ÷ Covers

B. Labor cost ÷ Sales

C. Sales ÷ Number of hours worked

D. Labor cost ÷ Number of hours worked

10 Which of the following would indicate how good a salesperson a server is?

A. Sales per cover
C. Total hours worked

B. Covers per hour
D. Average wage per hour

11 Which of the following would indicate how efficient a server is at turning over tables?

A. Sales per cover

B. Covers per hour

C. Total hours worked

D. Average wage per hour

12 If sales for the period are $113,000, and the number of hours worked by hourly employees is 290, what is the sales per labor hour for the operation?

A. $194.83
C. $389.66

B. $327.70
D. $427.22

79

Notes

The Capital Budget

7

After completing this chapter, you should be able to:

■ Explain the purpose of a capital budget.

■ Describe the process followed to prepare a capital budget.

■ Assess an operation's capital needs.

■ Evaluate different options for capital purchases.

■ Prioritize and plan capital purchases.

Test Your Knowledge

1 **True or False:** Major equipment that will be used for more than one year is considered a capital item. *(See p. 83.)*

2 **True or False:** Capital items are often referred to as furnishings, fixtures, and equipment. *(See pp. 82–83.)*

3 **True or False:** The capital budget is part of the overall operating budget. *(See p. 83.)*

4 **True or False:** It is not possible to accurately compare two different options for a capital purchase. *(See pp. 84–86.)*

5 **True or False:** Capital spending should be prioritized according to least expensive items followed by most expense items. *(See p. 87.)*

Key Terms

Capital budget

Capital item

Cost/benefit analysis

Economy study

Furnishings, fixtures, and equipment (FF&E)

Payback period

Rate of return

Return on investment (ROI)

Introduction

Every operation will have spending needs that fall outside of its daily costs of operation. At times, major purchases, such as those for replacement equipment or facility repairs, are necessary just to keep the operation in business. Other times, an operation might need to spend money on large projects like remodeling or expansion. Such work can be costly, but it can help an operation maintain its competitive edge. Improvements and upgrades that are carefully planned and budgeted for can help operations realize their profit potential and avoid becoming obsolete.

How does one plan for this spending? And how does a manager ensure that these major expenses do not negatively affect the operation's profit and loss report? The answers to these questions lie in the effective planning and use of a capital budget.

What Is a Capital Budget?

A **capital budget** is a spending plan specifically for major purchases that will be used over a long period of time. Such expensive purchases, which are commonly referred to as **furnishings, fixtures,**

Think About It...

How might the decision between leasing or purchasing a piece of equipment affect the capital budget?

and equipment (also known as FF&E), are known as **capital items.** Capital items require financial commitment that extends into the future. Generally, if the item being purchased is expected to last beyond one year, it would be considered capital items. Operations may specify actual limits for categorizing an item as a capital item. For example, any purchase over $500.00 might be a guideline.

It is important to note the difference between items included on the capital budget versus items that fall into the operating budget, which was discussed in Chapter 4. A capital budget *does not include* day-to-day operating expenses such as food, labor, rent, etc. Capital spending is not rolled up into an operation's profit and loss statements, as the substantial costs of capital items can cause the statements to be skewed.

Activity

How Variable Is the Cost?

For each of the budget items listed below, identify whether the item should be included in the capital budget (c) or the operating budget (o).

_____ **1** Monthly payments for leasing a dishwasher

_____ **2** New plumbing in the dishwasher area

_____ **3** Purchase of a new ice machine

_____ **4** Hiring a weekend hostess

_____ **5** Monthly payments for leasing a dishwasher

_____ **6** New plumbing in the dishwasher area

_____ **7** Purchase of a new ice machine

_____ **8** Hiring a weekend hostess

Preparing a Capital Budget

Preparing a capital budget is a fairly straightforward process. But it is important to understand that the more careful effort that is made during this process, the more efficient the budget will be. There are three essential steps in creating a capital budget: assessing capital needs, evaluating identified needs, and prioritizing and justifying the needs. A capital budget that has not gone through these important steps of analysis, prioritizing, and planning, runs the risk of being inadequate.

Step 1: Assess Capital Needs

The first thing managers must do when creating a capital budget is to evaluate the operation to determine what capital needs exist. *Exhibit 7a* lists some sample questions that managers should ask when evaluating the capital needs at their operation. The process of performing this evaluation results in a "wish list" of capital items for the operation.

Exhibit 7a

Assessing Capital Needs

Capital Category	Questions to Ask
Furnishings and fixtures	■ What repairs or replacements need to be made to furniture—such as chairs, tables, or countertops?
	■ Does anything require professional cleaning or replacement—such as drapery or carpeting?
Equipment	■ Has any equipment become obsolete or significantly behind in technology?
	■ Are there equipment pieces that are not running efficiently and/or need frequent repair?
	■ Can current equiptment keep up with forecasted production volumes?

Step 2: Evaluate Identified Needs

To address the capital needs of the operation, managers should compare several purchase options, as the best option is often not immediately clear. Once a list of capital needs has been prepared, each item on the list should be carefully evaluated in terms of a cost/benefit analysis. A **cost/benefit analysis** is a way of looking at the cost of purchasing an item in relationship to its purchasing potential cost savings. **Return on investment (ROI)** is a measurement of the financial benefits of a purchase as well. In other words, these analyses answer the question: how much is saved or earned in the long run by making the purchase? Answering this question aids a management team to make capital purchases that result in the most financial benefit to the operation. There are several options for performing cost/benefit analysis and ROI evaluations.

Rate of Return

The most common way to evaluate ROI is comparing the cost of an item in relationship to its potential cost savings. One technique used to evaluate return on investment is to calculate the anticipated rate of return. The **rate of return** is the relationship between the savings (or additional income) and the amount expended on the item. The formula used to calculate rate of return is:

Income or savings generated by project	$\div$	**Net amount invested in project**	$=$	**Rate of return**

Here is a simple example. A restaurant is considering purchasing a new dishwashing machine. In order to analyze the rate of return for this purchase, the financial information related to the purchase and potential cost savings need to be collected. This information is highlighted in *Exhibit 7b*. The manager has pulled together the information related to the value of the existing dishwasher, its remaining life expectancy, its value (if sold today), and the labor costs it takes to operate it. For the new dishwashing machine, the manager has collected information such as the price of the machine (including installation costs), life expectancy, value at the end of the expected life, and labor costs for its operation.

Exhibit 7b

Economy Study Evaluating Return on Investment

Existing dishwashing machine	**New dishwashing machine**
■ Has a book value of $5,000	■ Costs $12,000 installed
■ Could be expected to last five more years	■ Has an expected life of ten years
■ Could be sold now for $2,000	■ Has no expected salvage value after ten years
■ Results in annual operating expenses (largely labor) of $20,120	■ Requires fewer worker hours and additional supplies to operate, which results in annual operating expenses of $15,940

Based on the given information, the new dishwashing machine costs $12,000, and the old machine can be sold to recover $2,000. This results in a net investment of $10,000. What is the return for this $10,000 investment?

According to the information provided, the new dishwashing machine will result in a cost savings of $4,180 annually. This is figured by comparing the annual cost of operating the old machine ($20,120) to the annual operating costs for the new one ($15,940). So the rate of return is stated as a percentage.

In this example, the rate of return on investment is 41.8 percent, which is calculated as follows:

$4,180 ÷ $10,000 = .418 or 41.8%

An operation might have a standard guideline in place stating that capital spending with a rate of return of lower than 20 percent will not be approved.

Payback Period

Another technique used to evaluate and analyze possible capital expenditures is called the payback period. The **payback period** is the length of time it will take to recover the amount of an investment. Generally, the shorter the period to recover the funds spent on an item, the better investment it is. The formula to calculate payback period is:

| **Net cash outlay for project** | ÷ | **Annual net income (or savings) for project** | = | **Payback period** |

For the example in *Exhibit 7b* on the previous page, the investment is $10,000 and the return is $4,180. The payback period is then calculated as follows:

10,000 ÷ $4,180 = **2.39 years or approximately 2 years, 3 months**

Based on this information, the payback period is about two years and five months. This payback period can then be compared to those of other options to determine which option will result in the quickest payback period. It can also be compared to an operation-specific guideline. For instance, some operations might not approve capital spending on any item that has a payback period of longer than two years.

Economy Study

An **economy study** is a direct financial comparison of cost/benefit analyses two or more alternatives. Performing this comparison helps a manager determine which option is more economically advantageous. Some questions that can be answered by an economy study include:

- Which of several purchases should be made?
- Are extra features worth the cost?
- Should more expensive equipment be purchased?
- Is it financially desirable to replace equipment while it is still usable?

Activity

Capital Item Evaluation

A foodservice operator is contemplating the purchase of a new oven. The oven would cost $22,000 and have an anticipated life of ten years with no salvage value. The present oven could be sold for $5,000. If not sold, it is estimated to have a five-year life remaining with no salvage value. After calculating all savings from the new oven apart from depreciation, but including any additional expenses, it is estimated the new oven would result in a net savings of $4,000 per year.

Given this information, answer the following questions:

1 What is the payback period for the new oven? _____

2 What is the anticipated rate of return for the new oven? _____

Step 3: Prioritize and Justify the List of Items

Rarely can an operation finance all the capital items on its wish list. Instead, managers have to prioritize and justify the need to make each different purchase. Assigning these priorities also helps managers determine when to make the purchases, and in what order. However, there are some capital expenditures, such as a broken boiler or leaking roof, that must be made regardless of other considerations.

The highest priority must be given to the following:

- Items that pose a safety risk, either to customers or employees (broken or malfunctioning equipment, uneven flooring, etc.)

- Items that cause the operation to fall beneath local codes (fire codes, health regulations, etc.)

Outlining Capital Spending Plans and Timelines

Since it is usually necessary to make capital expenditures over a period of time rather than all at once, it is necessary to pre-plan when this capital spending will occur. This, of course, involves the priority or necessity of the project, as well as forecasting when funds for the projects will be available. There may be years when, in order to accumulate funds for larger purchases, none or only minor capital purchases are scheduled. It may also be necessary to make unplanned capital expenditures, such as an unexpected furnace replacement.

Exhibit 7c

Capital Spending Schedule

Year	New dishwashing machine
2008	Replace walk-in refrigerator
2009	Repaint dining room
2010	Repave parking lot
2011	Install new serving counter

Exhibit 7c is an example of a capital spending schedule.

Exhibit 7d lists some of the capital items that have been prioritized and planned for in a hospital dietary department, and shows a capital spending plan outlining priorities as well as a simple spending timeline for the items needed.

Like any budget, capital budgets must be approved by the individuals who authorize such spending for the operation. This could be the owner of a restaurant, an area manager for a small chain, or the corporate purchasing department for a large chain. Review and approval are necessary to ensure the capital budget is realistic and appropriate.

Funds for capital budgets can come from earnings, depreciation, or new investment. Operations can also plan for future capital purchases by putting aside a set amount on a regular basis. In addition, several businesses specialize in financing new construction, real estate purchases, and renovation projects for the foodservice industry. The federal government also administers funding resources to help individuals and groups, such as women and minorities, and small business owners.

Exhibit 7d

Sample Capital Spending Plan

	Each	Total	Estimated Date of Payment	Justification
Priority: Urgent/Essential				
■ Tray cart for floor service	$1,450	$1,450	Immediate	The present cart is inoperative and cannot be fixed, and a cart must be reloaded, slowing service
■ Fire extinguisher system over broiler hood	$2,000	$2,000	October	Local fire code to require this by November 1
Priority: Economically desirable				
■ Computer system	$8,000	$8,000	May	Estimates are that it could pay for itself in three years
Priority: Generally desirable				
■ Four stainless-steel shelf units (4) for bakery storeroom	$500	$2,000	June	Enhanced quality appearance and organization of storage

Bob's Garage

Kelly is the owner of Bob's Garage, a popular beer and burger restaurant in the business district of a large town. Lately, Kelly has noticed that lunch sales have drifted steadily downward, although she has not had any customer complaints and has a great, experienced staff. She thinks this trend might be due in part to the new 1950s-style diner that opened up around the corner. It has been in operation for only three months and is very eye-catching, with lots of neon and shiny chrome.

Kelly takes a look around Bob's Garage. She notices several tables with coasters under them to keep them from wobbling, and eighty out of the 125 vinyl chairs have tears or cigarette burns on them. In addition, the skylights need professional cleaning, and the sign outside needs replacement. She also received a notice from the fire department that each tenant in her building would need to install a sprinkler system within ninety days in order to satisfy new fire code requirements.

Kelly puts together some cost estimates on these projects.

Option	Cost	Comments
New chairs	$33 per chair; $2,640 to replace 80 chairs; $4,125 total to replace all 125 chairs	Chairs come with one-year warranty for replacement
Reupholstering chairs	$7 per chair; $560 to repair 80 damaged chairs	Upholstery comes with a six-month warranty
Skylight cleaning	$125 × 6 skylights = $750	
New sign	$2,150 installed	
Sprinkler system	$1,800 installed	
Project total	$8,825	Includes 125 new chairs

Kelly contacts the local bank and is approved for a small business loan of only $5,000. Given this information, answer the following questions:

1. How would you recommend Kelly use the $5,000 on capital improvements for Bob's Garage?

2. Justify the recommendations. Why did you choose some options over others?

Summary

Every operation has spending needs that fall outside of its daily costs of operation, such as improvements and upgrades. A capital budget is a spending plan for major purchases that will be used over a long period of time. Such expensive purchases, commonly known as furnishings, fixtures, and equipment (FF&E), are called capital items. A capital budget *does not include* day-to-day operating expenses.

To create a capital budget, you must first determine what capital needs exist. This results in a "wish list" of capital items, which you must then evaluate. Options for performing such analysis include analyzing costs and benefits for different options and comparing them, or calculating the payback period or the rate of return.

Then, you must prioritize and justify the need for each capital purchase. Assigning priorities helps you determine when to make the purchases, and in what order. Priority must be given to items that address a safety risk or ensure the operation meets local codes.

Since capital expenditures typically must be made over time, you must pre-plan when this spending will occur. This involves determining the priority or necessity of the project, as well as forecasting when funds for the projects will be available. Like any budget, capital budgets must be approved by the appropriate individuals in the operation.

Review your Learning

1 A capital budget is often used to

A. track profits or losses over time.

B. measure controllable supply costs.

C. check the operating budget for accuracy.

D. plan for major improvements and enhancements to the operation.

2 What is the first step when creating a capital budget?

A. Create a list of capital needs.

B. Perform a cost/benefit analysis.

C. Outline the capital spending timeline.

D. Prioritize and justify capital purchases.

3 What does the acronym "FF&E" stand for?

A. Fix it, file it, and evaluate it

B. Furbish, finish, and expand

C. Furnishings, fixtures, and equipment

D. Functions, furniture, and emergencies

4 An economy study is the

A. financial comparison of two purchase options.

B. determination of the length of time a piece of equipment should last.

C. calculation of the relationship between the savings and the amount expended.

D. calculation of the length of time it will take to recover the amount of an investment.

5 Of the following, which would have the highest priority on the capital budget?

A. Sidewalk repair

B. Drapery cleaning

C. Upgraded printers

D. Complete remodel of operation

Notes

Field Project

Financial Procedures Audit

This field project is designed to give you a glimpse of how the financial management processes and procedures in this Review Guide are applied in a real-world foodservice environment. This project will give you an in-depth "reality check" regarding financial management practices in a single operation.

The Assignment

Select a foodservice operation—it can be either commercial or noncommercial, and from any segment of the industry. Get approval from the operation's manager to perform a basic audit of the financial management processes currently in place at the operation. This audit will entail researching brief questions related to financial management practices, viewing sample forms and documents, and observing employee practices. It is estimated that you will need at least ten hours of time to interact with the operation manager and staff to collect the information you need.

Prepare a report that includes the following three sections:

1 Current Financial Management Practices

2 Analysis/Evaluation of Current Financial Management Practices

3 Recommendations for Future Enhancements

Use the following questions as guidelines to get you started.

1 Current Financial Management Practices

Managing Cash at the Operation

☐ What procedures exist for processing guest payments?

☐ How are employees trained in these procedures?

☐ What tools are in place to help spot counterfeit currency?

☐ How does the management staff monitor the handling of cash by employees?

☐ What procedures are in place to ensure cash is stored securely?

☐ What tools or forms are used for cash register reconciliation?

☐ What tools or forms are used for bank deposit preparation?

Managing Payables and Receivables

☐ What procedures are in place for managing accounts payable?

☐ Does a chart of accounts exist for the operation? If not, how are invoices categorized?

☐ Who is responsible for authorizing payment of invoices?

☐ What procedures are in place for managing accounts receivable?

☐ How are credit terms for house accounts determined?

☐ How does the operation identify and collect past-due accounts receivable?

Exploring Costs

☐ Which operating costs are controllable? Which are noncontrollable?

☐ Which operating costs are variable? Semi-variable? Fixed?

Financial Procedures Audit *continued from previous page*

Preparing the Operating Budget

☐ How are sales revenue forecasts prepared? How accurate are they?

☐ How are food costs forecasted? How accurate are they?

☐ How are labor costs forecasted? How accurate are they?

☐ Does the operation use a master schedule? If not, how is the hourly employee schedule determined?

☐ Examine an operating budget for one period. How is it organized?

Introduction to Cost Control

☐ How are sales and cost data collected?

☐ How are sales and cost data analyzed? What are the actual figures compared to?

☐ Which costs are more likely to be out of line?

☐ What corrective actions are most often needed to bring these costs back into line?

☐ What is the target food cost percentage?

☐ How is food product waste recorded and calculated?

☐ What is the target labor cost percentage for the operation?

☐ What productivity ratios are commonly used to analyze labor costs? How are these calculated?

The Profit and Loss Report

☐ How often are profit and loss reports created?

☐ What is the procedure for collecting information to generate profit and loss reports?

☐ What does the profit and loss report look like? How is the information organized?

☐ How are profit and loss reports analyzed?

The Capital Budget

☐ Is there a capital budget in place? If so, what items are included?

☐ How is the capital budget prepared?

☐ What information is considered when planning for capital spending (return on investment, priorities, etc.)?

☐ What items are being considered for future capital budgets?

2 Analysis/Evaluation of Current Financial Management Practices

☐ How effective are the practices and tools that are currently in place?

☐ Where is the operation at risk of losing money?

3 Recommendations for Future Enhancements

☐ What changes or improvements would you recommend? For the short term? For the long term?

☐ What would it cost to implement these enhancements? Propose a sample budget for implementing these recommendations.

Index

Index

H

historical costs, 68–69
historical sales information, 60, 67
house accounts, 24

I

identification, proof of, 9, 10
insurance, 33, 34
Internal Revenue Service (IRS), 49
inventory, 72
investment, 84–86
invoice, 21–23, 25
    authorization of payment, 22
    categorization, 21–22
    payment of, 22–23

L

labor cost, 33, 35, 42–48, 68, 69, 73–77
labor cost percentage, 73–74
    analysis, 74
late fees, 26
lease, 33, 36
line item review, 67, 68
loss, 40, 58

M

master schedule, 47
menu, 33
monitoring, 2–3
mortgage, 33
moving average, 42

N

noncontrollable costs, (see costs)

O

operating budget, 40–49, 50–51, 66, 69, 83
operational records, 41–42
overages, 13
overhead, 42

P

payables, 21–24
payback period, 86

Payment

payment, 5, 7–11, 24
    accounts payable, 21–24
    accounts receivable, 26
    cash, 5–8, 11
    non-cash, 9–11
    safeguarding of, 11
    tableside, 11
payroll, 44–48
payroll cost, 73
personal checks, 9
petty cash, 14
point-of-service equipment (POS), 3, 12, 42, 57, 67
pricing, 33
production reports, 42
production sheet, 41
profit, 40, 58, 68
profit and loss, 40, 49
profit and loss report (income statement), 56–58, 59, 60, 83
    analysis, 59–60
    organization, 57
purchases, 70, 84–88, 89

Q

quick-change artists, (see con artists)

R

rate of return, 85–86
receipt, 12, 13
receivables, 25–26
reconciliation, 12–13
rent, 36
return on investment (ROI), 84–86
revenue, 40, 41

S

salary, 35
sales, 35, 36, 41–44, 57, 60, 67, 71, 73
    analysis, 67–69
    data, 67
sales per cover, 75–76
sales per labor hour, 74–75
sales reports, 12
sales tax, 3
schedule, 33, 35, 45–48, 68, 69, 77
scheduling software, 48
secret shoppers, 3

semivariable

semivariable costs, (see costs)
service schedule, 44–45
shrinkage, (see food product waste)
signature, 9
skimming, (see bleeding)
staff issues, 2–4, 12, 13, 74–77
    crew schedule, 48
    gratuity (tip), 4
    theft 3
standard costs, 68–69
standards, 44–46, 60, 68, 74
subtotal, 3–4
suppliers, 21, 23
surveillance system, 3, 12

T

taxes, 13, 49, 58,
    sales tax, 3
theft, 3, 7, 13
tip, (see gratuity)
total, 7
traveler's checks, 9
    security features, 9

U

utilities, 33

V

variable costs, (see costs)
variances, 13, 59, 60, 67, 69
vendor discounts, 23
vouchers, 23–24

W

wages, 35, 45, 46
waste, (see food product waste)